The Alchemy Of Hope

Cycle A Sermons
Based on Second Lessons
For Lent and Easter

James D. Monnett, Jr.

CSS Publishing Company, Inc.
Lima, Ohio

THE ALCHEMY OF HOPE

FIRST EDITION
Copyright © 2022
by CSS Publishing Co., Inc.

Published by CSS Publishing Company, Inc., Lima, Ohio 45807. All rights reserved. No part of this publication may be reproduced in any manner whatsoever without the prior permission of the publisher, except in the case of brief quotations embodied in critical articles and reviews. Inquiries should be addressed to: CSS Publishing Company, Inc., Permissions Department, 5450 N. Dixie Highway, Lima, Ohio 45807.

Library of Congress Cataloging-in-Publication Data:

Names: Monnett, James, 1969- author.
Title: The alchemy of hope : cycle A sermons based on the second lessons for Lent and Easter / James D Monnett.
Description: Lima, Ohio : CSS Publishing Company, Inc., 2022.
Identifiers: LCCN 2022017705 (print) | LCCN 2022017706 (ebook) | ISBN 9780788030604 (paperback) | ISBN 9780788030611 (adobe pdf)
Subjects: LCSH: Lenten sermons. | Easter--Sermons. | Lectionary preaching. | Common lectionary (1992). Year A.
Classification: LCC BV4277 .M65 2022 (print) | LCC BV4277 (ebook) | DDC 252/.62--dc23/eng/20220602
LC record available at https://lccn.loc.gov/2022017705
LC ebook record available at https://lccn.loc.gov/2022017706

For more information about CSS Publishing Company resources, visit our website at www.csspub.com, email us at csr@csspub.com, or call (800) 241-4056.

e-book:
ISBN-13: 978-0-7880-3061-1
ISBN-10: 0-7880-3061-2

ISBN-13: 978-0-7880-3060-4
ISBN-10: 0-7880-3060-4

Contents

Ash Wednesday: 2 Corinthians 5:20-6:10
Firm In The Waves... 5

Lent 1: Romans 5:12-19
A Royal Blue Home 9

Lent 2: Romans 4:1-5,13-17
Raw Power 14

Lent 3: Romans 5:1-11
Breathe Grace 19

Lent 4: Ephesians 5:8-14
Shine Bright 23

Lent 5: Romans 8:14-25
Oh, The Places You'll Go! 28

Palm Sunday : Philippians 2:1-13
Rejoice Greatly 34

Passion Sunday: Philippians 2:1-13
Jumped The Tracks 39

Maundy Thursday: 1 Corinthians 11:23-26
Magic 44

Good Friday: Hebrews 4:12-16; 5:7-9
Wounds 48

Easter: Acts 10:34-43
God Raised 53

Easter Day: Colossians 3:1-4
Resurrection Power 58

Easter 2: 1 Peter 1:3-9
Evelyn Finds Hope 62

Easter 3: 1 Peter 1:17-23
The Alchemy Of Awkward 67

Easter 4: 1 Peter 2:19-25
Tennessee Red Mud 71

Easter 5 (Mother's Day): 1 Peter 2:2-10
Bactine® 76

Easter 6: 1 Peter 3:13-22
Baptized By Cool Water.. 80

Ascension of the Lord: Ephesians 1:15-23
Christ's Body On Earth 87

Seventh Sunday of Easter: 1 Peter 4:12-16, 5:6-11
Lava Faith 92

Ash Wednesday
2 Corinthians 5:20-6:10

Firm In The Waves

So we are ambassadors for Christ, since God is making his appeal through us; we entreat you on behalf of Christ, be reconciled to God. For our sake he made him to be sin who knew no sin, so that in him we might become the righteousness of God.

As we work together with him, we urge you also not to accept the grace of God in vain. For he says,

"At an acceptable time, I have listened to you, and on a day of salvation I have helped you."

See, now is the acceptable time; see, now is the day of salvation! We are putting no obstacle in anyone's way, so that no fault may be found with our ministry, but as servants of God we have commended ourselves in every way: through great endurance, in afflictions, hardships, calamities, beatings, imprisonments, riots, labors, sleepless nights, hunger; by purity, knowledge, patience, kindness, holiness of spirit, genuine love, truthful speech, and the power of God; with the weapons of righteousness for the right hand and for the left; in honor and dishonor, in ill repute and good repute. We are treated as impostors, and yet are true; as unknown, and yet are well known; as dying, and see — we are alive; as punished, and yet not killed; as sorrowful, yet always rejoicing; as poor, yet making many rich; as having nothing, and yet possessing everything.

Have you ever stood waist-deep in Lake Michigan? You stand in the waters with your back to the shore, looking out at the horizon. Water, water, water, then a thin line and sky. Small waves move the water against your skin.

Larger waves may require you to jump.

How high are the waves that you are facing?

In an Ash Wednesday worship service, as we dab a cross on your forehead or your hand with palm frond ashes mixed with olive oil, we often say: *For dust you are and to dust you shall return.* (Genesis 3:19)

Palm fronds remind us of Jesus riding the donkey into Jerusalem, with the crowds waving palm fronds and shouting "Hosanna," which means savior.

The olive oil is considered holy. When they were nomadic, living in tent communities, the ancient Hebrew community would have one tent for worship. At night, the priest or an elder would set an oil lamp on the edge of the worship tent that would burn olive oil all night long.

In the darkest part of the night, if anyone felt alone or in need of God, a glance at that lamp's burning flame would be an instant reassurance. God is here.

Imagine the ash of a palm frond in a paste with olive oil. It is poignant to remember last year's Palm Sunday's palm fronds are now ash. When we have that ash paste dabbed on our forehead, there will be a visible reminder life is short.

Life is short.

For dust you are and to dust you shall return.

Do the waves seem high? Does life seem like it is too complicated? Do the problems we face seem overwhelming?

The story of Adam and Eve eating the forbidden fruit in the Garden Eden is a powerful story that reminds us that we all turn from God. We can judge Adam and Eve by thinking, "You had one job. Don't eat that fruit." But when we look back at our lives, we can pick out four or five times we did the same thing:

- Why did I say that?
- Why did I do that?
- Why didn't I speak up?
- Why didn't I stand up in that situation?
- Why did I hurt the people I love?

Love your neighbor as yourself. These ancient words that Jesus spoke are powerful. Yet, we don't always do that. We shouldn't judge Adam and Eve for disobeying God as we do so as well. Love your neighbor as yourself sounds easy.

Jesus quotes Leviticus in a passage where God speaks to Moses, giving directions on how the new people, recently rescued from slavery in Egypt, should build their society. Leviticus 19:16-18:

> *You shall not go around as a slanderer among your people, and you shall not profit by the blood of your neighbor: I am the Lord. You shall not hate in your heart anyone of your kin; you shall reprove your neighbor, or you will incur guilt yourself. You shall not take vengeance or bear a grudge against any of your people, but you shall love your neighbor as yourself: I am the Lord.*

What would our community look like if we lived out this command to love people?

Maybe we wouldn't be standing in the water facing the waves alone in such a community.

We could link arms and stand firm in the waves.

On Ash Wednesday, walking through our everyday life at work, school, or home, we will see people with ashes on their forehead or the back of their hands. We will know that we are not alone. We do stand in the waves together. We stand across human denominational lines. Denominations mean no more to God than national borders mean to the birds in the air or the fish in the sea.

Ash Wednesday begins the forty days to Maundy Thursday. That gives us forty days to renew our focus on the Triune God: God, Jesus, and the Holy Spirit.

In ancient times, these forty days were a time for the new believers to learn the essentials of the Christian faith. More than this, it was a forty-day journey to know Jesus better. Growing closer to Jesus is what we do today in Lent. We take forty days to grow in our faith — a time to prepare for the celebration of Easter and the resurrection of our Lord Jesus Christ.

To begin Lent, we have this one day — Ash Wednesday — to remember that life is short. We must value it highly and enjoy it fully:

So we are ambassadors for Christ, since God is making his appeal through us; we entreat you on behalf of Christ, be reconciled to God. For our sake he made him to be sin who knew no sin, so that in him we might become the righteousness of God.

As "ambassadors for Christ," may we use these forty days to draw closer to the Lord God Almighty. May we know that we are part of one worldwide community of believers seeking to build a better world. A world where we are not alone. A world where we can stand firm in the water, no matter what waves we face. We will meet the waves together — arm in arm.

Praise the Lord. God's name be praised.

Prayer:
Gracious and loving God, we find our lives overwhelming sometimes. Be with us this day and through these forty days so that we may experience the fullness of a loving community. May we learn to love ourselves. May we learn to love our neighbors. May we always love you, Our God. In Jesus' name, Amen.

Lent 1
Romans 5:12-19

A Royal Blue Home

Therefore, just as sin came into the world through one man, and death came through sin, and so death spread to all because all have sinned — sin was indeed in the world before the law, but sin is not reckoned when there is no law. Yet death exercised dominion from Adam to Moses, even over those whose sins were not like the transgression of Adam, who is a type of the one who was to come.

But the free gift is not like the trespass. For if the many died through the one man's trespass, much more surely have the grace of God and the free gift in the grace of the one man, Jesus Christ, abounded for the many. And the free gift is not like the effect of the one man's sin. For the judgment following one trespass brought condemnation, but the free gift following many trespasses brings justification. If, because of the one man's trespass, death exercised dominion through that one, much more surely will those who receive the abundance of grace and the free gift of righteousness exercise dominion in life through the one man, Jesus Christ.

Therefore, just as one man's trespass led to condemnation for all, so one man's act of righteousness leads to justification and life for all. For just as by the one man's disobedience the many were made sinners, so by the one man's obedience the many will be made righteous.

Over Christmas break, the high school youth mission team painted a parsonage for a small independent Baptist church in a small town on an island in the Florida Keys.

The house was tiny but well-loved by the young pastor, his wife and their three small children. It was on the back of the church property. The street next to the parsonage had the backs of the large oceanfront homes that make the Keys famous.

In the mornings, as we painted, people honked and waved as they drove past. Standing on her small porch with her infant child in our arms, the young mother told the teenagers that sometimes she heard people make fun of the house for its peeling khaki-colored paint.

"It's so hard," she said as her child fussed on her shoulder.

Mom was not talking about the house. As a new pastor in his first call, the pastor had thrown everything he had into this small church with its food and clothing pantries, as well as a weekly Wednesday night meal for sixty-plus hungry people.

This was not the life this young mother may have envisioned from her suburban upbringing at the big, packed church outside Jacksonville.

This young family lived on the edge of poverty themselves.

Poverty is food insecurity, low wages, families living where the *money runs out before the month ends*, and so much uncertainty.

The apostle Paul writes this letter from his Roman cell to the Christian house churches in Asia Minor (modern Turkey). Paul wants to share good theology to encourage the churches to be faithful in the midst of difficulty as they work for the kingdom of God.

Today's reading builds a history showing that God's intent for the world began with creation and continues through the faithfulness of Abraham and Sarah, Isaac, Jacob, Moses, Debra, Ruth, Boaz, King David, the prophets, and to Jesus. The apostles' ministries to and with these Christian churches are part of this good work even now.

Life's hardships are not new. God understands. God is moving in the world to transform the world through Jesus Christ:

But the free gift is not like the trespass. For if the many died through the one man's trespass, much more surely have the grace of God and the free gift in the grace of the one man, Jesus Christ, abounded for the many.

The free gift of grace found in Jesus Christ is not like the trespass — not like the sins — of Adam and Eve disobeying God. We have the "free gift" of redemption "in the grace" of Jesus Christ.

By following Jesus, we are helping to move the world toward redemption.

The Christian faith is one of grace. This grace, this hope, is a gift through Jesus:

Therefore just as one man's trespass led to condemnation for all, so one man's act of righteousness leads to justification and life for all. For just as by the one man's disobedience the many were made sinners, so by the one man's obedience the many will be made righteous.

Jesus is this "one man." Through Jesus' resurrection over death, God is reclaiming — transforming or transfiguring — the world to be the kingdom of God. A place where people find community and belonging.

Each day the youth mission team painted that house. Each day the painting transformed the house into gleaming royal blue beauty.

Some of the youth used their free time before dinner to help with the family's housework. They carried the overflowing laundry basket from the tiny house to the church's ministry building laundry.

Two sophomores sat at the kitchen table, coloring with the children.

The bathroom got cleaned because, "My mom said I have to clean a bathtub every Tuesday over Christmas break or I might lose my skills."

Yes, the young mother rolled her eyes as he said it, but she did direct him to the Comet® and cleaning rags.

All of this came without any direction from our youth leaders. It came from a heart of care.

As the forty days of Lent stretch ahead of us, that bathtub might help us understand how we could experience this Lent.

In early Christian times, the forty days were a time of preparation for baptism. They became a time for adult confirmation to prepare to enter into the Christian community of the church. Today, Lent is a time of reflection and often a recommitment to faith practices from Bible reading and prayer to serving others.

What inspired that junior to decide he should give the bathroom a good cleaning? He wanted to help, and cleaning bathrooms was one of his chores back home. An adult may have chosen decorum over offering to clean the bathroom, but teenagers often go with the impulse. For this young family, they welcomed the offer.

What if our Lent could follow the impulse to help with the household chores? What if we didn't focus on giving something up for this Lent but instead focused on helping?

Just pause to consider how you could help your school, your church, around your neighborhood or community? They can be anything.

Here are some brainstormed ideas to get you thinking:

- Do some snow removal for the family down the street.
- Offer to help the church sextons (custodians) with a project they need an extra set of hands to do.
- Clean the basement.
- Sort your closet, making a box of clothes for the local clothes closet.
- Start a church or school collection for winter coats, hats, boots, and gloves.
- Find the Comet® and clean the bathrooms in your home.
- Pick a charity and write them a check equal to a week's worth of groceries in your home — or a gas tank's worth.
- Organize a group of volunteers for a workday to help the residents in an assisted living center, homeless shelter, or a local elementary school.

What ideas do you have that would utilize your skills or gifts?

We could use these forty days of Lent to make the world a bit better by doing a few small acts of goodwill.

Can you picture such a Lent of service? Maybe by Holy Week, we would have a bright, royal blue home. Amen.

Prayer:
Loving and kind God, thank you for all you are and all you do to make this world better. Guide us into service. Show us where we can make a difference. Inspire us to discover the joy of serving others. We love you, Lord, Amen.

Lent 2
Romans 4:1-5, 13-17

Raw Power

What then are we to say was gained by Abraham, our ancestor according to the flesh? For if Abraham was justified by works, he has something to boast about, but not before God. For what does the scripture say? "Abraham believed God, and it was reckoned to him as righteousness." Now to one who works, wages are not reckoned as a gift but as something due. But to one who without works trusts him who justifies the ungodly, such faith is reckoned as righteousness.

For the promise that he would inherit the world did not come to Abraham or to his descendants through the law but through the righteousness of faith. If it is the adherents of the law who are to be the heirs, faith is null and the promise is void. For the law brings wrath; but where there is no law, neither is there violation.

For this reason it depends on faith, in order that the promise may rest on grace and be guaranteed to all his descendants, not only to the adherents of the law but also to those who share the faith of Abraham (for he is the father of all of us, as it is written, "I have made you the father of many nations") — in the presence of the God in whom he believed, who gives life to the dead and calls into existence the things that do not exist.

On January 23, 1973, the Eldfell volcano erupted on the island of Heimaey, off the coast of Iceland.

The eruption spewed ash to the south. The majority of islanders were able to evacuate by fishing boats. A small crew of brave police and firemen stayed behind to protect the town and the harbor.

They worked to divert the destruction for six months by spraying seawater on the lava flow to harden and divert new lava away from the harbor.

These brave women and men worked for six months to protect their home and their community.

Instagram videos showed floodwaters in China. In one, a raging river flowed through a town. As we watch, the flooding river struck a pedestrian bridge and swept it into the flow. The person recording on their phone followed the metal bridge as it bobbed and swirled down the river. We watched as it was carried away.

We are left wondering how people will get from one side of the river to the other.

We are left wondering about the raw power of the flooding river.

And we may wonder about the person up on the roof recording this with their cell phone. Why are they still there? What are they feeling? Are these people watching that power and feeling it break their hearts as their town is on the brink of disaster?

Our cell phone rings on a Saturday afternoon. It is our sister. Mom is gone. It was sudden. We don't know what caused it — heart attack, stroke, or something else. She asks, "Can you come home now?"

Eldfall is raw power. The flooding river is raw power.

Death in any of its forms is raw power capable of changing our world. It can happen without any warning. One moment we are out back on our deck reading *Sports Illustrated*, and the next — Tornado warning. Flood watch. Volcano warning.

The cell phone rings and our life changes forever. Abraham's life changed when God called upon him to go and found a nation. Romans 4:2-3:

> *For if Abraham was justified by works, he has something to boast about, but not before God. For what does the scripture say? "Abraham believed God, and it was reckoned to him as righteousness."*

Abraham wasn't justified, wasn't declared worthy for anything he did. Instead, God looked upon Abraham and saw righteousness. God saw a good heart.

Abraham was far from perfect. And we can draw comfort from this, for we are far from perfect too.

God's love is the raw power that is indescribable and incomprehensible.

We don't know how our world may change on a dime. But we can rely on God's love when the world changes; God's love is raw power itself. We can stand against anything in God's love.

God's love carries us through disasters. We will not be alone when the rivers and lava flow. God is with us when we face cancer, the miscarriage, the crumbling of a marriage, or the death of our life partner after sixty years together.

We know that sometimes bad stuff happens, and our world changes. But we stand secure knowing that God's love is *still* here.

Yes, the world can change on a dime, and sometimes it isn't natural disasters, accidents, or medical conditions that hurt.

Sometimes it is other people.

I could make a list here as well, but let's just take a moment and remember how we have seen others hurt by people. Or, if the one hurt is us, let's take this moment and breathe in the grace of God's indescribable love.

We don't know why God allows it, but we know that by Jesus' agony on the cross, God feels the hurt too. God weeps too. The Apostles' Creed affirms that Jesus descended to hell, and three days later, he rose again. Standing for three days in hell, Jesus knows how we feel when we've experienced life-altering hurt by the ones who choose evil.

Life can change on a dime.

In the stories of Abraham, the apostle Paul wants us to understand how much God loves us. God loved Abraham and Sarah, calling them to follow him not because they were perfect or sinless. God looked upon them and saw a reflection of God-self. God saw righteousness.

God sees us as his children and looks beyond our sin — sees through our inadequacies — and sees hope. God sees a future and offers us this redemption through Jesus Christ.

Jesus Christ, like God's love, is raw power.

Romans 4 is complicated theology that the apostle Paul has written in letter form to encourage the new Christian house churches in Achaia (Greece) and Asia Minor (Turkey). Paul wants the new Christians to know that they are descendants of Abraham and Sarah, not by ethnic blood but by the love that leads Jesus to the cross so that all who believe in him may have life and have it abundantly. Romans 4:16a:

> *For this reason it depends on faith, in order that the promise may rest on grace and be guaranteed to all his descendants...*

If we have faith and trust in God, grace is guaranteed to us, for we are descendants of Abraham by the blood of Jesus.

We don't have to be of Hebrew descent or become Jewish, as some preached in Galatia. In Jesus, we are all descendants of Sarah and Abraham because of Jesus. Romans 4:17:

> *as it is written, "I have made you the father of many nations) in the presence of the God in whom he believed, who gives life to the dead and calls into existence the things that do not exist.*

Raw power — God's love is raw power. Abraham and Sarah are our theological parents because the blood of Jesus has redeemed us. God chose them because of their righteousness, and, in Jesus, God claims us too.

Redemption is offered to everyone — a gift of grace.

But...

It is so hard to accept this love and grace when we are in pain. When people have hurt us, it is nearly impossible to *let go, let God*. It feels impossible to choose love when we are struggling, even impossible to let God love us.

How can we let God love and heal us when we are hurting?

Maybe we don't have to expect healing to be easy.

Maybe we should accept that healing is sometimes incremental, with two steps forward and one painful step back. Paul speaks of letting a God into our lives who (Romans 4:17b):

> *gives life to the dead and calls into existence the things that do not exist.*

Healing the hurts in our lives seems impossible. We are a rugged, mountainous island covered with plains of brown grasses of pain, hurt, and worry. The raw power of the volcano gives us a glimpse of the raw power of God's healing.

God can break through our lives and change us for good. Jesus can transform us. The Holy Spirit can heal us.

Praise be to God is all things, Amen.

Prayer:
Creator God, we put our trust in you. Bring the raw power and resurrection of love over the hurt, peace over worry, grace over sin. Lord, we put our trust in you. Be here with us where we are so that we will know we are never alone, Amen.

Lent 3
Romans 5:1-11

Breathe Grace

Therefore, since we are justified by faith, we have peace with God through our Lord Jesus Christ, through whom we have obtained access to this grace in which we stand; and we boast in our hope of sharing the glory of God. And not only that, but we also boast in our sufferings, knowing that suffering produces endurance, and endurance produces character, and character produces hope, and hope does not disappoint us, because God's love has been poured into our hearts through the Holy Spirit that has been given to us.

For while we were still weak, at the right time Christ died for the ungodly. Indeed, rarely will anyone die for a righteous person — though perhaps for a good person someone might actually dare to die. But God proves his love for us in that while we still were sinners Christ died for us. Much more surely then, now that we have been justified by his blood, will we be saved through him from the wrath of God. For if while we were enemies, we were reconciled to God through the death of his son, much more surely, having been reconciled, will we be saved by his life. But more than that, we even boast in God through our Lord Jesus Christ, through whom we have now received reconciliation.

Ten days ago, I stood on the sand and looked up.

The boulder was massive. It had cleaved off the cliff above and sat before us like a throne. It was over twenty feet high and covered with vegetation. Behind it, I could see the face of the cliff itself.

The sounds of the surf crashing against the cliff fill my ears.

I looked over at my buddy, Adar. He gave me a thumbs up. Without speaking, we both knew. This sight was magnificent.

God made this magnificent scene. I was in awe: filled with amazement at the beauty — the tremendous power of creation.

Have you been to places on this earth where you have to stop moving and stand in awe of the creation?

I remember standing before Old Faithful, the most famous geyser at Wyoming's Yellowstone National Park — feeling blown away.

Or in Vermont, standing on the wooden walkway covered with spray at the waterfall known as The Flume.

We were standing knee-deep in an unnamed river with two members of our youth group in the middle of The Great Smoky Mountain National Park. Forest, mountains, flowing water.

God made all of this.

We were sitting on the dunes over in Holland, Michigan, at Tunnel Park, looking at Lake Michigan on a summer day. It was utter peace and beauty.

God made all of this.

Standing in the sand boulder in front of me, off the Bahamas' Eleuthera Island, marveling at God's creation, and reflecting on God's grace. Each time I breathed in, compressed air transferred from my scuba tank, through my regulator, past my teeth, and into my lungs.

My dive buddy Adar floated gently two feet off the bottom of the Atlantic Ocean. I stood on my flippers in the sand, 65 feet down, marveling at God's grace.

In my first scuba diving class, our instructor Dave observed a truth that I believe stands right alongside the Apostle Paul's views on faith and grace.

Dave said you have to remember something when scuba diving: you only get three strikes underwater before getting hurt — *and the first strike is that you are not a fish.*

Before you jump off a boat to scuba dive, you check your equipment. Then your buddy checks it a second time. You do the same for his equipment.

Every breath you take underwater comes from the air on your back.

This is what God's grace is.

Have you ever tried to define grace? The online dictionary, *Merriam-Webster.com,* defines grace as "unmerited divine assistance given to humans for their regeneration or sanctification."[1]

Wow, that is a mouthful.

This is grace.

I can share with you everything about what it is like to step off a boat with a scuba tank on your back. That first hit of cold water into our wet suit. Swimming away so others can enter. The amazingly wrong feeling of sinking — watching the water slide over our mask until we are underwater — *and breathing*.

I can tell you of the descent, of swimming amongst the boulders. I can describe what it is like to swim through tunnels made by haphazard boulders and the view of a six-foot barracuda hovering evilly at the end of the tunnel.

I can describe it all. But you won't truly understand scuba diving through my descriptions.

All our air is on our back (buddy-breathing is a learned technique, but too scary to think about).

Total dependence.

Ahh, this is grace.

Every bit of grace we experience comes from God.

Paul writes Romans to the Christian churches in Rome. This letter is a treatise on faith, grace, and Jesus. It is a testimony. It is hope. It is encouragement.

Descending 65 feet into the ocean is a trust-fall a hundred times scarier than any corporate training trust-fall. Paul (Romans 5:6-8):

> *For while we were still weak, at the right time Christ died for the ungodly. Indeed, rarely will anyone die for a righteous person—though perhaps for a good person someone might actually dare to die. But God proves his love for us in that while we still were sinners Christ died for us.*

---

1 "Grace", Merriam Webster Dictionary. Accessed September 17, 2021. https://www.merriam-webster.com/dictionary/grace.

For while we were still weak, at the right time Christ died for the ungodly.

The New International Version says: *When we were still powerless, Christ died for the ungodly.*

Merriam-Webster gives us "regeneration and sanctification" for grace.

All three definitions proclaim that by Jesus' death and resurrection, we can experience a community with God that not just nourishes us like a good meal, but that is essential to us like the air we breathe.

Take a deep breath with me. Go ahead, breathe it all. Exhale knowing that God's grace is here within us.

We all know how to breathe air. What if we could get to the point of letting God's grace through Jesus Christ live inside us like the air we breathe?

Just that easy. Just that holy. Just that beautiful.

Breathing grace is appreciating the mountain and the waterfall. Grace infuses us whether we sit high on the dune at sunset or gently float on the sandy bottom of the ocean.

God is just this magnificent.

Amen.

Prayer:
O holy one, you are magnificent. You have given this fantastic creation for us to enjoy and nourish. Walk and swim with us as we live our lives fully in your glory. God, we live in awe of you. We are thankful, Amen.

Lent 4
Ephesians 5:8-14

Shine Bright

For once you were darkness, but now in the Lord you are light. Live as children of light— for the fruit of the light is found in all that is good and right and true. Try to find out what is pleasing to the Lord. Take no part in the unfruitful works of darkness, but instead expose them. For it is shameful even to mention what such people do secretly; but everything exposed by the light becomes visible, for everything that becomes visible is light. Therefore it says,
'Sleeper, awake!
 Rise from the dead,
and Christ will shine on you.'

When we live in the dark, what would we give for a light?

When we take a cave tour, the guides always have that moment when they ask us to turn out our flashlights down deep in the cave. Each light clicks off; it gets darker. Then we are down to two lights. One more flashlight clicks off.

Then we wait. It is always that one kid who wants the moment in the literal spotlight. But we don't care because we both want them to turn out the light and — *please don't turn out the light.*

What if the light never comes back on? Maybe we are in the limestone caves of Wyandotte, Indiana, or far below the New Mexico desert in Carlsbad Caverns. We are down deep, and everything is dark. What if the light doesn't come on again?

We hope that one kid doesn't press the button to extinguish the last light.

Then she presses the button.

Darkness — utter darkness. Hold your hand up. Go ahead. Right now, wherever you are, hold up your hand. Imagine that dark cavern. Imagine you cannot see your hand right here. Touch your nose. Yup, your hand is there, but you cannot see it.

Can you imagine your hand right in front of your nose, and that you *cannot* see it?

This is Ephesus before the missionaries from Jerusalem from the Roman province of Palestine came to the Roman province of Achaia, which is what we call Greece. This is Ephesus before the apostle Paul himself comes to Ephesus to preach the good news of the gospel of Jesus Christ.

Look at our hands. We cannot see our hands. We live in a land of deep darkness. John wrote in his gospel (1:5): *The light shines in the darkness, and the darkness has not overcome it.*

This is Ephesus, that Greek city under Roman rule.

Did you know Ephesus is home to one of the *Seven Wonders of the Ancient World*?

The Temple to Artemis is one of these seven wonders: the grandest edifice in all of Ephesus. Commercial life revolves around the temple. Priests sacrifice animals inside it and then sell the same animals in the butcher's market. Are we going to eat the burger of the cow offered to the Greek god of the Hunt — Artemis? Is the act of our eating this meat a sign we are paying tribute to the most powerful god of our city?

The money flows into the temple of Artemis, and then it flows to the community as loans for farmers' seeds and tools for the carpenter or the potter. Does this money carry the taint of Artemis? Is she present in all that we do?

Yes, the people of Ephesus live in darkness.

Not only does Ephesus have the Temple of Artemis, but according to archeological sources and the Book of Acts, Ephesus is the occult capital of the Roman Empire.

Need to buy a spell for an abundant crop? Someone can help us in Ephesus. Need an enchantment so that we can have a baby? Ephesus is the place to go. Do we need an evil curse for the landowner who won't pay our fair wage? Go to Ephesus.

In Ephesus, they have written the spells, enchantments, and curses down together in the *Book of Names*. In the Book of Names are all the gods, lesser demigods, and demons available to help us with whatever part of the darkness we cannot handle on our own: loneliness, financial struggle, unemployment, or a broken heart. We are struggling with cancer, leprosy, heart disease, Covid-19 — there is help in Ephesus. Come to Ephesus, and for a few coins, we can buy a spell to help with the darkness.

Hold up your hands again. When people have no hope — when we have no hope, when we cannot see the fingers in the front of our face — what happens?

We look for the light.

When we are struggling in the darkness, it can be challenging to walk by faith.

The Christian churches of Ephesus are struggling to walk by faith. They need support and encouragement. They need light.

The apostle Paul, who founded the Christian churches in Ephesus, knows about darkness. Before meeting Jesus, Paul went by the name Saul, and he was a Pharisee who persecuted Christians for teaching heresy to the Jewish community around Jerusalem.

Then one day, Saul met the risen Jesus (Acts 9:3-7):

> *Now as he was going along and approaching Damascus, suddenly a light from heaven flashed around him. He fell to the ground and heard a voice saying to him, "Saul, Saul, why do you persecute me?" He asked, "Who are you, Lord?" The reply came, "I am Jesus, whom you are persecuting. But get up and enter the city, and you will be told what you are to do." The men who were traveling with him stood speechless because they heard the voice but saw no one.*

In Damascus, Jesus called a believer named Ananias and sent him to Saul to preach the good news, for Jesus had great plans for the new Paul, to preach to all the Gentiles (non-Jewish people). Acts 9:17-19:

> *So Ananias went and entered the house. He laid his hands on Saul and said, "Brother Saul, the Lord Jesus, who appeared to you on your way here, has sent me so that you may regain your sight and be filled with the Holy Spirit."*

> *And immediately, something like scales fell from his eyes, and his sight was restored. Then he got up and was baptized, and after taking some food, he regained his strength.*

The apostle Paul knew three days of darkness.

When Paul met the light of the world through Ananias' preaching, the risen Jesus restored his sight. Paul was the one who went out to preach the good news of the Lord Jesus Christ.

The reborn Paul brought light to those who walked in darkness. Paul, with his acolytes, founded the Christian church in the occult capital of the world in Ephesus. (Acts 19) Later, one of those acolytes will write this letter to the Christian house churches in Ephesus encouraging them.

> *God put this power to work in Christ when he raised him from the dead and seated him at his right hand in the heavenly places, far above all rule and authority and power and dominion, and above every name that is named.*

Jesus is above every name. The name of Jesus is the name above all names. Jesus, the light of the world, is set above the powers of darkness.

Jesus is a star in a dark sky.

Ephesians 5:13 and 14:

> *but everything exposed by the light becomes visible, for everything that becomes visible is light.*

Even if we live in complete darkness, deep in the cave of despair, know that light is coming. Jesus is near, and the light will pierce the darkness. Help is on the way.

Isaiah 9:2:

> *The people who walked in darkness have seen a great light; those who lived in a land of deep darkness — on them, light has shined.*

Isaiah 42:6-8:

> *I have given you as a covenant to the people, a light to the nations, to open the eyes that are blind, to bring out the prisoners from the dungeon, from the prison those who sit in darkness. I am the Lord, that is my name;*

What a great proclamation: **I am the Lord, that is my name**. Jesus is a name above all names. A star high in the sky.

We feel the starlight crack the darkness. The light breaks through all the darkness that causes us suffering and pain. In Jesus, we have hope.

Even in darkness, we hope for Jesus. We hope for better days. We hope for a better world. Since we put our trust in Creator God, we know that change is coming.

We remember the Christmas story with the Star of Bethlehem lighting the way to the Savior. Just as the wise men with their large entourage followed the light of the star to see Jesus, we too follow the light, trusting in him with our whole heart.

Who is this light of the world? In Isaiah 9:6-7, we meet Jesus:

> *For a child has been born for us, a son is given to us; authority rests upon his shoulders; and he is named Wonderful Counselor, Mighty God, Everlasting Father, Prince of Peace. His authority shall grow continually, and there shall be endless peace*

Amen.

Prayer:
Gracious and loving God brings the joy of Christmas Eve into our hearts this day. Lift us so that we know that the love you have for us is present at all times, even when we cannot see it. Help us to use our minds to believe when our hearts are heavy. Lord Jesus, we will trust in you to be with us at all times, Amen.

Lent 5
Romans 8:14-25

Oh, The Places You'll Go!

For all who are led by the Spirit of God are children of God. For you did not receive a spirit of slavery to fall back into fear, but you have received a spirit of adoption. When we cry, "Abba! Father!" it is that very Spirit bearing witness with our spirit that we are children of God, and if children, then heirs, heirs of God and joint heirs with Christ — if, in fact, we suffer with him so that we may also be glorified with him.

I consider that the sufferings of this present time are not worth comparing with the glory about to be revealed to us. For the creation waits with eager longing for the revealing of the children of God; for the creation was subjected to futility, not of its own will but by the will of the one who subjected it, in hope that the creation itself will be set free from its bondage to decay and will obtain the freedom of the glory of the children of God.

We know that the whole creation has been groaning in labor pains until now; and not only the creation, but we ourselves, who have the first fruits of the Spirit, groan inwardly while we wait for adoption, the redemption of our bodies. For in hope we were saved. Now hope that is seen is not hope. For who hopes for what is seen? But if we hope for what we do not see, we wait for it with patience.

My older brother John gave me Dr. Seuss' children's book, *Oh the Places You'll Go!* for my college graduation. In the fall, I would move to Chicago to go to seminary for the ministry. I thought the Dr. Seuss book was a fantastic gift.

John wrote nice words in the front. On the back page, he had taped some cash with a note explaining that the money was for "when you need a break — whether it's a concert, a show, or a trip to the beach — and you feel you can't afford it — *now you can.*"

Now you can — are there words more potent than these?

Now you can.

We live in a world where it is easy to believe that we can't.

In May, a group of us from our church went down to Cass Community Social Services[2] in Detroit to help renovate an old four-story brownstone that Cass Community had bought from the City of Detroit. They were renovating the old building to make apartments for people to live in as they move from the shelter.

Homelessness is one of those areas where it is easy to believe we can't. We can't make a difference. We can't help change people's lives. The problem is too big. The problem is too vast.

Also, the problem is in Detroit. Sometimes suburban Detroit church people act like Detroit's poverty issues are not our problem. We let ourselves believe that because Detroit's problems are too significant, we can ignore them and focus on the homeless and food insecure in our suburbs.

Each winter, when the rotating shelter brings the cots to our churches to host the overflow men from the local homeless shelter, we realize that we can make a difference. And if we partner with organizations like Cass Community, we can make a difference for Detroit as well.

As we meet the men in the rotating shelter, something else changes. We get to know the people themselves. They stop being "homeless people" and become who they are — people.

Cass Community is working for solutions, though maybe not a solution to *all* homelessness. Still, the renovation of that brownstone will be a solution for the twelve to fourteen families and individuals who will no longer be homeless.

Now we can.

In the third floor apartment, Philip and I took turns standing over a hole in the bathroom floor, looking down on the second floor apartment below. We swung sledgehammers to break out a cast iron bathtub. It was hard work — also, lots of fun.

[2] For more information on Cass Community Social Services, visit their website at casscommunity.org.

Now we can.

Some will say this isn't a local mission because it is not Ann Arbor where we live. But I love Detroit as I have loved Cleveland, and it is a place our church can live out the gospel.[3]

Detroit is a place where Paul might have said, and this is the *New Century Bible* version of our reading (Romans 8:18-21):

> *The sufferings we have now are nothing compared to the great glory that will be shown to us. Everything God made is waiting with excitement for God to show his children's glory completely. Everything God made was changed to become useless, not by its own wish but because God wanted it and because all along there was this hope: that everything God made would be set free from ruin to have the freedom and glory that belong to God's children.*

I love this: "Everything God made is waiting with excitement for God to show his children's glory completely."

The word "completely" also means "fully" as in we see the world darkly, but "then we will see face to face" as Paul writes in 1 Corinthians.

The Cass Community is waiting with excitement for God to show his children's glory fully. What is this "glory"? It is a new bathroom with a solid new floor. It is an apartment for a previously homeless family who can now say, "Now we can."

Oh, the places they'll go from there.

The Christian Education committee at church has overseen three or four different day trips to Detroit for mission work. We have had four or five kids sign up — total.

Why?

Our youth are busy. They have a student government, sports — school and travel clubs, choirs as time-consuming as varsity football, theater, dance recitals, and so much more. They carry heavy course loads with many AP classes, labs, and multidiscipline classes like humanities that culminate, for some, in a trip to Italy to see how it all fits together.

3 I grew up in Solon, a southeast suburb of Cleveland, Ohio. Go Browns!

They have many family commitments, and they must get to know their extended family — family is still how we know our history and practice love.

Into the midst of all this, though, our youth are seeking God.

When we offer one-day mission trips, we think we are offering youth an easy way to do it, but they can't get away from their school and sports commitments for a whole day. The coaches, cast mates, and robotics team don't understand.

Our students can get away for an extended mission trip easier than for a single workday.

A junior on travel hockey said his coach told him to take the week and do good for the world. They would miss him, but his spot was secure. He should do something for others.

That same coach would never let him miss a hockey game to go to Cass Community in Detroit for a workday. Can't you go to Cass on a different day?

In 2011, our high school mission team went to Montego Bay, Jamaica, to work at the Caribbean Christian Center for the Deaf.[4] We had 29 high schoolers who took ten days away from everyday life to love God and serve others.

Each night in Jamaica, we worshiped. Worship involved singing together, scripture reading, and a short message. Some of the school's youth worshiped with us. Our students worked to sign the worship to them.

Two of the boys would sing with us with their hands. They sang in silence and spirit.

After worship, we broke into four small groups. My small group met down the hill outside on the front porch of the school's clinic. We had a beautiful view of the lights of Montego Bay far below us. One night, we could see the outline of a cruise ship on the ocean. Seven lizards shared their porch with us, hanging on the ceiling, the posts, and sometimes hopping right next to us. They kept the insects away.

We sat in the dark, using a flashlight for reading.

One night the small group talked about how cool it was to meet the school's students. They laughed about how hard it was

---

[4] For more information about the Caribbean Christian Center for the Deaf, visit www.cccdjamaica.org.

to learn signs. Someone reminded the others that the Jamaicans do not use American Sign Language, but Jamaican Sign Language. Similar, but different.

Then the story came out that one of the older local students had signed to our student that though the school hosted many high school mission teams, very few take the time to meet them.

Few mission teams from the United States take the time to try to communicate with the students and adult teachers by sign.[5]

Mission teams should want to learn some signs to talk with the CCCD community. But learning sign language involves trial and error. It requires care, patience, and the willingness to get it wrong. It also entails for everyone to participate in order to learn this new language.

In our small group, the youth shared how much it meant to meet students their age but who lived differently. And who live in a country where parents can harm children with disabilities when they are infants or toddlers because they are considered useless. These youth shared how lucky they were to have the Caribbean Christian Center for the Deaf find them and invite them to live on one of CCCD's three campuses: at Montego Bay, Knockpatrick, or the Kingston campus. On any of these campuses, they could live, learn, and be valued here.

At the Knockpatrick campus, in the hill country, is the Jamaican Deaf Village, created by CCCD in 2002. It is an entire village where anyone who speaks Jamaica Sign language can live and work together in village-wide industries to support the community. It is a whole community of partially or wholly deaf people and hearing people who sign.

As this youth spoke about how thankful she was to be here experiencing this community at the CCCD Montego Bay campus, my heart broke as the Holy Spirit convicted me of my failure.

This was my second mission trip to CCCD, yet I had not made an actual connection with a student or adult from the school.

The next day, I had my first halting conversation with a high school student who would take the time with my terrible sign

---

5   Nearly everyone child, youth, adult who live at the CCCD is deaf.

language. How could I have lived my life without speaking with a child of God who speaks this language?

Our students made friends with the students of the school. Some continued to speak with each other by Facebook or Twitter after the trip.

Paul wrote that God is at work in the world.

Whether we are at Cass Community, in the church, here in our living rooms, at the Knockpatrick village, sitting in our office, or working on the CCCD campus in Montego Bay, we can be living out our hope in God.

We are living out our hope in God. A hope that God will redeem us, redeem the world, and make a difference in what we cannot see or hear.

For God is at work in the world.

Now we can be at work, too. Now we can be at work in the world.

Oh, the places we'll go to together.

Amen.

Prayers:
Wherever we go, you are there. Dear Jesus, show us the way to go where you are leading. Help us to trust in you. Guide us to the place we can serve in your name. Bring us the courage to learn some sign language and find new people to laugh with as we expand our world. We thank you for your presence in our lives, Amen.

Palm Sunday
Philippians 2:1-13

Rejoice Greatly

If then there is any encouragement in Christ, any consolation from love, any sharing in the Spirit, any compassion and sympathy, make my joy complete: be of the same mind, having the same love, being in full accord and of one mind. Do nothing from selfish ambition or conceit, but in humility regard others as better than yourselves. Let each of you look not to your own interests, but to the interests of others. Let the same mind be in you that was in Christ Jesus, who, though he was in the form of God, did not regard equality with God as something to be exploited, but emptied himself, taking the form of a slave, being born in human likeness. And being found in human form, he humbled himself and became obedient to the point of death — even death on a cross. Therefore God also highly exalted him and gave him the name that is above every name, so that at the name of Jesus every knee should bend, in heaven and on earth and under the earth, and every tongue should confess that Jesus Christ is Lord, to the glory of God the Father.

As a 25-plus year pastor, I have a lot of books on my shelves. I have read most of them. One section is reserved for the "to be read" books. For years, I carted around five seminary books that I could not gear myself up to read.

These books were not easy to read. They were hard.

They might have been helpful if I could have figured out all the jargon and big words the scholars use. Sometimes the seminary professors choose books that are beyond their students.

How many years should I move those five books?

A decade was it. Those books went to a local academic used bookstore.

We are lucky that Matthew, Mark, Luke, and John wrote the stories of our Lord Jesus Christ so that readers can understand his life, death, and resurrection.

The writers of the New Testament wrote it to be shared, to be read, to be discovered. More than this, the New Testament helps us not just talk about Jesus but meet Jesus. We will meet him and give our lives to him. Jesus will save us.

The gospel itself is not hard to understand. The gospel, the good news, reveals Jesus to us. As Paul says, they show the Jesus who:

> *though he was in the form of God,*
> *did not regard equality with God*
> *as something to be exploited,*
> *but emptied himself,*
> *taking the form of a slave,*
> *being born in human likeness.*
> *And being found in human form,*
> *he humbled himself and*
> *became obedient to the point of death —*
> *even death on a cross.*

Paul understands the truth of Jesus, and he shares it with us.

Jesus humbled himself and was obedient to God's will to love people regardless of what they might do.

Jesus knew his most prominent critics — the Jewish religious leaders — were centered in Jerusalem. These men knew the Roman governor Pontius Pilate. They had Pilate's ear.

Going to Jerusalem was risky.

Loving others can be risky. Jesus goes to Jerusalem, into the belly of the whale, to show love to everyone, even people who fear him. People who hate.

Jesus still goes to Jerusalem: to show the world what real love is.

As Jesus entered Jerusalem on the back of a donkey, the crowds came to love and praise Jesus. They waved palm fronds. They yelled, "Hosanna!" It was a triumphant entrance to Jerusalem.

In a few short days, the soldiers would arrest Jesus. Pilate would question him and have him beaten. Through it all, Jesus showed love. Pilate ordered Jesus' execution. Jesus kept loving them.

At the religious leaders' demands, Pilate sentenced Jesus to crucifixion. Jesus would hang to death on a cross at Golgotha, which is Aramaic for the skull and in Latin is Calvary. In English, Golgotha is simply "Place of the Skull."

Even here, Jesus does not turn to power and violence. He is love personified.

On Golgotha will be Jesus' death on a cross. Will Jesus love them still? Will Jesus love his accusers still? Will he love… still?

He humbled himself and
became obedient to the point of death —
even death on a cross.

I didn't comprehend those complicated theology books, but I understand the story of the Passion of Jesus — this story of Jesus' crucifixion.

Sometimes what is necessary isn't complicated analysis and intellectual somersaults. Sometimes simplicity is best.

Simplicity.

This Sunday — which may be Palm Sunday or Passion Sunday or both — is a time to consider the whole Holy Week.

Imagine we are holding a palm frond. Feel its smoothness. Rub its length over our fingertips. Imagine that palm parade outside Jerusalem.

Jesus entered Jerusalem, and crowds made of believers, disciples, and well-wishers came out to greet him as he entered. They — we wave palm fronds. We shout Hosanna!

The ride into Jerusalem on the donkey fulfills the words of the prophet Zechariah who said (Zechariah 9:9):

Rejoice greatly, O daughter Zion!
Shout aloud, O daughter Jerusalem!
Lo, your King comes to you:
triumphant and victorious is he,

> *humble and riding on a donkey,*
> *on a colt, the foal of a donkey.*

Prophecy fulfilled.

The crowds gathered much as we gather in our churches. Some firm, devout believers. Some with questions still unanswered. Others only go along to see what is going on and to see what might happen.

It isn't much to stand on a roadside and wave a palm frond at a visiting person. It isn't much to yell, "Hosanna in the highest" at a visiting king.

What becomes important is how we see ourselves relative to this king.

The sign on the cross will read, "This is Jesus, the king of the Jews." Is Jesus our king? Is he our savior?

The Romans put the placard on the cross as the charge for why they were crucifying Jesus. Pilate is executing Jesus for claiming to be a king. In a Roman province, no one is king but the emperor. To claim to be a king is to be a political revolutionary.

Is this Jesus?

Whoever heard of a political revolutionary whose platform and practice is love?

Jesus is such a revolutionary.

This is the Jesus entering Jerusalem on a donkey like the judges would ride when they visited the towns of early Israel. The judges rode donkeys because horses are not native to Israel and would be brought by the Philistines years later. When the judges rode the donkey, they did so back before Israel had human kings. The judges rode donkeys back when only God was king.

Now Jesus is on a donkey. Jesus is God and king.

The cross placard is only half-right. "King of the Jews," yes. It would be even more descriptive if it said "King of kings" or "Lord of lords." Maybe even "King of all!"

The people who wrote the placard and hammered it into the cross on which Jesus died did not believe. He was not their king. He was a nobody to them.

Yet...

They were still somebody to Jesus. He died on that cross for them as much as he did it for us and everyone in between.

At the death of Jesus, a Roman centurion felt the earthquake, saw the sky darken, and felt the tremor of hope in Jesus in his heart. Matthew 27:54:

> *Now when the centurion and those with him, who were keeping watch over Jesus, saw the earthquake and what took place, they were terrified and said, "Truly this man was God's Son!"*

Holy Week is a significant spiritual time as we breathe in the Jesus stories of Palm or Passion Sunday, Maundy Thursday, Good Friday, Holy Saturday, to the trumpets of Easter worship.

Jesus is significant to us. Jesus is king and Savior and Lord to us.

Praise the Lord; God's name be praised. Amen.

Prayer:
Dear Jesus, this Palm Sunday inspires us to come to the parade with an open, trusting heart. May we be people with love for everyone around us. May we be people of peace at services this Holy Week. Fill us with love for Jesus on Easter Sunday. Lord Jesus, show us how to share our joy and be genuinely glad we are all together for Easter morning. Show us your love. Show us your glory, dear Jesus, Amen.

Passion Sunday
Philippians 2:1-13

Jumped The Tracks

If then there is any encouragement in Christ, any consolation from love, any sharing in the Spirit, any compassion and sympathy, make my joy complete: be of the same mind, having the same love, being in full accord and of one mind. Do nothing from selfish ambition or conceit, but in humility regard others as better than yourselves. Let each of you look not to your own interests, but to the interests of others. Let the same mind be in you that was in Christ Jesus, who, though he was in the form of God,
   did not regard equality with God
   as something to be exploited,
but emptied himself,
   taking the form of a slave,
   being born in human likeness.
And being found in human form,
   he humbled himself
   and became obedient to the point of death —
   even death on a cross.

Therefore God also highly exalted him
   and gave him the name
   that is above every name,
so that at the name of Jesus
   every knee should bend,
   in heaven and on earth and under the earth,
and every tongue should confess
   that Jesus Christ is Lord,
   to the glory of God the Father.

> *Therefore, my beloved, just as you have always obeyed me, not only in my presence, but much more now in my absence, work out your own salvation with fear and trembling; for it is God who is at work in you, enabling you both to will and to work for his good pleasure.*

Haiti, Syria, Rwanda, Ferguson, and fifty more places in the world have strife.

Kneeling during the national anthem, the Detroit riots, vaccination status, white supremacy marches, MSNBC, Fox News, ICU beds, student debt, climate science, and fifty more happenings have strife.

Strife strikes closer to home as well:

- The co-worker who is always looking emotionally spent.
- The classmate who is sullen and angry.
- Your brother and his wife who — "We can't talk about it."
- The friend at girls' night out who just shakes her head when you ask how she is.
- Your parents who are not talking and always angry.

People all around us are living in strife.

Strife is such a perfect word. It sounds harsh to the ear. It feels disruptive to the heart.

People we know are living in strife. They are living in pain. Their lives have jumped the tracks.

Remember those *Hot Wheels*® orange tracks?

When my daughter was young, and we were visiting my mom's home, I so wanted to show my daughter how awesome it was to race *Hot Wheels* down the track into some nice S-curves and 180s — maybe a loop or two, if we still had them.

No loops, but the rest of the orange tracks were in a box in the basement. I showed Kate how they fit together. We attached the vise holding the top of the track to a patio table.

We depressed the launch button. The car shot down the track into the first turn and jumped the track.

We tried multiple times. We changed the track. We changed cars. We tried different plastic connectors.

The cars kept jumping the track.

The world seems to be jumping the track. How can we seek peace when our car is airborne?

Isn't this what happens to our relationships when we jump the track? Isn't this what our lives feel like some of the time? No matter what we do, our lives are jumping the track.

Late last night, The Romans soldiers arrested Jesus. He was in the garden with Peter, James, and John, praying. Arrested while peacefully praying is life jumping the track.

Then Jesus was questioned and beaten.

Peter, who always seemed to be the guy with all the good answers, out by a cooking fire, denied knowing Jesus three different times after Jesus' arrest.

We saw Peter after. He is miserable. We all are. Some of us, the men and women who follow Jesus, the so-called disciples, have already taken off. Everyone is afraid. We understand why they fled. It is understandable. What if the soldiers come to arrest all of Jesus' followers?

Now it is morning, and Jesus is on the hill called Golgotha — the Skull.

Soon they will nail Jesus to the cross. They will crucify Jesus between two criminals.

Mary, Jesus' mother, John the beloved, and Mary Magdalene are all up close to Jesus. They are praying hard for a miracle.

The Roman soldiers go about crucifying these three men. This is just business, just orders. Something is desperately wrong when killing people by nailing them to the cross is normal. For the Roman Empire, death is routine.

Will this day be routine?

As Jesus' followers, all night, we have been wrestling with what it all means. Where is God? Will God intervene? Will Jesus die? What about love? What about all of Jesus' teachings, the kindness, and the miracles?

What is to come after today?

They crucify Jesus on Golgotha. From the cross, Jesus prays for the Roman soldiers, for the crowds, for everyone (Luke 23:34): "Father, forgive them; for they know not what they are doing."

One of the criminals recognizes Jesus in a way that so few ever did (Luke 23:42-43):

> *Then he said, "Jesus, remember me when you come into your kingdom." He replied, "Truly I tell you, today you will be with me in paradise."*

The apostle Paul, writing in this letter to the Greek churches in Philippi, will use this poetry to describe Jesus:

> *who, though he was in the form of God, did not regard equality with God as something to be exploited, but emptied himself, taking the form of a slave, being born in human likeness. And being found in human form, he humbled himself and became obedient to the point of death — even death on a cross. Therefore God also highly exalted him and gave him the name that is above every name, so that at the name of Jesus every knee should bend, in heaven and on earth and under the earth, and every tongue should confess that Jesus Christ is Lord, to the glory of God the Father.*

This is Jesus — the one to whom we should give our hearts.

Our lives may jump the tracks, our world may be full of strife, but Jesus is the name above every name. Jesus' name is above all strife.

Friends, do we hear this? Do we believe this?

Jesus' name is above all strife, all conflicts, all distress. Jesus is the name above every name.

We will continue to face strife, and our lives may jump the tracks, but Jesus is next to us. We will not go off the rails alone. We are never alone again.

And someday... someday:

at the name of Jesus every knee should bend, in heaven and on earth and under the earth, and every tongue should confess that Jesus Christ is Lord, to the glory of God the Father.

In the name of the Father, the Son, and the Holy Spirit, Amen.

Prayer:
Our hearts are broken this day, dear Lord, as we remember Jesus on the cross. Be with us. In your mercy, hear our cry and do not leave us. Our lives often jump the tracks as the world can be overwhelming. Be with us, dear Lord. Be with us in everything. We put our trust in you, Amen.

Maundy Thursday
1 Corinthians 11:23-26

Magic

For I received from the Lord what I also handed on to you, that the Lord Jesus on the night when he was betrayed took a loaf of bread, and when he had given thanks, he broke it and said, "This is my body that is for you. Do this in remembrance of me." In the same way he took the cup also, after supper, saying, "This cup is the new covenant in my blood. Do this, as often as you drink it, in remembrance of me." For as often as you eat this bread and drink the cup, you proclaim the Lord's death until he comes.

As kids in the middle of winter, we got dressed up and drove to the Palace Theater in downtown Cleveland. My dad was super excited. We were seeing Harry Blackstone Jr, the son of The Great Blackstone, whom my dad had seen as a kid. The Great Blackstone invented, with Thomas Edison's help, the floating light bulb trick. That light bulb and the Cassadaga Cabinet were the first two magician props accepted by the Smithsonian.[6]

Dad was over the moon for us to see the Great Blackstone's son.

I had tried my terrible hand at magic. Not sure if this was before or after seeing Blackstone. But I had my plastic magic top hat from which I could magically produce stuffed animals! I was always spilling milk in the basement as I tried to master that trick.

In my seat, I leaned forward, mesmerized by the illusions, sounds, and dazzle of it all. And then Blackstone disappeared, only to be replaced by a real live Bengal tiger!

The show has blown my mind. We spend days talking about it; how did they do that?

---

[6] The Cassadaga Cabinet, also called the Cassadaga Propaganda, is a Harry Blackstone Sr. magic trick where a slate board in a cabinet magically writes answers to questions asked of audience members.

Blackstone has many astounding magic tricks, but what feels like magic is what God does with God's mercy and forgiveness.

The real magic is what God does with love.

On Maundy Thursday, we will soon gather around the communion table and remember. We will not forget how Jesus gathered with his disciples around the table after he washed their feet. We will remember that Jesus has invited each one of us — Jesus has invited *all* of us — to his table to eat and drink with him, to know that no matter what we have done, we are loved.

The apostle Paul's says in this famous wedding passage in 1 Corinthians 13:1-3:

> *If I speak in the tongues of mortals and of angels, but do not have love, I am a noisy gong or a clanging cymbal. And if I have prophetic powers, and understand all mysteries and all knowledge, and if I have all faith, so as to remove mountains, but do not have love, I am nothing. If I give away all my possessions, and if I hand over my body so that I may boast, but do not have love, I gain nothing.*

In verse 2, Paul says that even if you can do the so-called complicated spiritual gifts like speaking in tongues or speaking prophesies — which means showing people what God is up to — which is no small gift — none of this matters, if we do it without love. Even if we understand all mysteries and knowledge, if we are the smartest person in the room but do not have love, we are nothing.

If we come to the Lord's table on this night and do so without love for those around us, we are… human. Human and in need of Jesus.

Paul's not talking about a fleeting love or a shallow love. He's not talking about the love an angel might have, sitting on a big fluffy cloud while playing an acoustic guitar and singing Stevie Wonder's "You Are the Sunshine of My Life."

This love that Paul is talking about is for **the real world**: — the three degrees, ice on the road; rain whipping across the Texas roads; Go Bears, Win Lions; my best friend is in a hospital bed;

our car won't start; the furnace is acting up; the pipes have frozen; our beloved child *won't stop crying.*

Paul is talking about a love that moves up to *be loving.*

Love is patient. (1 Corinthians 13:4-7) Love is kind. Love is not envious. Love does not tell you how right I am or how amazing I am because I am loving.

Love is not arrogant. Love is not rude — we should stop on this one and let it sink into us.

Love does not insist it is right; it does not insist on its own way.

Love is not irritable. It is not resentful — why do they have so many great things while my car won't start in this cold?

Love is not happy when people screw up.

Love likes the truth even when it is difficult.

> *Love bears all things, believes all things, hopes all things, endures all things.* (1 Corinthians 13:7)

Let's hear verse 7 again but in an upside-down world. Love endures everything, even the worst day we have had. **Love hopes all things.** On that terrible day, love knows it is going to get better. Love believes all things — good is going to come out of this big bad. Love endures our worst day.

Remember who was at the table with Jesus. Judas had eaten this bread and had drunk of this cup. Jesus welcomed Judas to his table. Judas was at the Lord's table. He was welcomed.

All are welcome at Jesus' table.

Jesus says in 1 Corinthians 11:24-26:

> *"This is my body that is for you. Do this in remembrance of me." In the same way he took the cup also, after supper, saying, "This cup is the new covenant in my blood. Do this, as often as you drink it, in remembrance of me." For as often as you eat this bread and drink the cup, you proclaim the Lord's death until he comes.*

When we gather at the Lord's table, when we have communion, we are one community. We are one people unified and redeemed by the bread and the cup. We are united in Jesus' love.

For love bears all things — love is going to carry us through it all. How do we know this? We trust in God, who is love. We trust that *love never ends*.

Paul says, "now we see in a mirror dimly." (1 Corinthians 13:12) We see in the "mirror dimly" because at this time, these are metal mirrors, and every bend causes the mirror to give a distorted picture. When we look at ourselves in a metal mirror, we see a distorted view of ourselves. God does not see a distorted view of us.

God sees us as we are: God's children.

We can sit at this table and see Judas and judge him, but we see the distorted picture. Jesus sees with eyes of hope. Jesus sees Judas with all Judas' misplaced hope that Jesus is a warrior waiting for the right moment to raise the sword and lead the armies of God against Rome. Judas sees a distorted Jesus.

Jesus doesn't see distortion. Jesus sees Judas as a child of God — one who is welcome at the table.

Jesus sees us all with our broken, sinful lives. Jesus sees us and knows we do not understand love. And Jesus loves us anyway.

The most powerful magic we will ever experience is that God, through Jesus, puts this love in our hearts through the movement of the Holy Ghost.

We all have it. At this communion table, we affirm that Jesus is our Lord and Savior.

Friends, the table is set. Jesus invites us to come. Come find a seat next to Andrew, beside Judas, across from James; let's eat and drink and know this love that flows through Jesus into our hearts.

Let us pray...
Dear Jesus, we accept your invitation to come and sit at the table with you. We know we are not worthy of anything we have done or said. We know we are welcome because all are welcome. Dear Jesus, we love you, and we thank you with our whole hearts for all you do for us. Amen.

Good Friday
Hebrews 4:12-16; 5:7-9

Wounds

Indeed, the word of God is living and active, sharper than any two-edged sword, piercing until it divides soul from spirit, joints from marrow; it is able to judge the thoughts and intentions of the heart. And before him no creature is hidden, but all are naked and laid bare to the eyes of the one to whom we must render an account.

Since, then, we have a great high priest who has passed through the heavens, Jesus, the Son of God, let us hold fast to our confession. For we do not have a high priest who is unable to sympathize with our weaknesses, but we have one who in every respect has been tested as we are, yet without sin. Let us, therefore, approach the throne of grace with boldness, so that we may receive mercy and find grace to help in time of need.

In the days of his flesh, Jesus offered up prayers and supplications, with loud cries and tears, to the one who was able to save him from death, and he was heard because of his reverent submission. Although he was a son, he learned obedience through what he suffered; and having been made perfect, he became the source of eternal salvation for all who obey him...

When I lived in Hyde Park, in the south section of Chicago, I would be hit up by homeless people at least three times every day walking to seminary class or the university's library. Over time, I came to know the guy at 57th and Kenwood and the other guy by Eduardo's pizza by name. However, their names are gone from memory nearly thirty years later. When I passed them, I often gave them coins or some dollar bills. Other times I didn't.

Friends would say, "Don't give money. They're only going to drink it."

That may have been true, but I like myself better as a person who sometimes shows compassion in the face of not enough facts.

Our Good Friday reading tells us that the Word of God — the Bible — is (Hebrews 4:12):

> *living and active. Sharper than any two-edged sword, it penetrates even to dividing soul and spirit, joints and marrow; it judges the thoughts and attitudes of the heart.*

And then in verse 13:

> *Nothing in all creation is hidden from God's sight. Everything is uncovered and laid bare before the eyes of him to whom we must give account.*

What we do is always visible. Visible to God and visible to us. We know what we've done. We know what choices we've made. We know when we've been compassionate and when we've been heartless.

When we've been gossiping about someone and later find out they overheard or that our supposed confidant wasn't so confidential? How do we face the friend after we've been talking about them? How do we feel?

Doesn't the guilt wash over us like water out of the bathtub? But it's not going back into the bathtub. The water is a mess on the floor.

We can't undo our mistakes.

Do we hear that? We can't undo our mistakes. And the guilt we experience is powerful.

A guilty heart is painful.

On Good Friday, this day, when we look at the cross, we feel the guilt of our sins and our faults. A sloshing bathtub of knowing — *knowing* — we are not worthy of Jesus' great love for us.

The Bible knows us. Listen to these words from both testaments:

Psalm 34:18

The Lord is near to the broken hearted, and saves those who are crushed in spirit.

Jeremiah 31:33-34

This is the covenant which I will make with the house of Israel, says the Lord: I will put my law within them, and I will write it upon their hearts; and I will be their God, and they shall be my people. I will forgive their evil deeds, and I will remember their sin no more.

And John 3:16-17

For God so loved the world that God gave his only son, that whoever believes in him should not perish but have eternal life. For God sent the Son into the world, not to condemn the world, but that the world might be saved through him.

God intends for us to have forgiveness. God gave us a way through the guilt, sin, and destructive behaviors we find ourselves returning to time and time again.

An unknown author tells the following story of a child who was having trouble controlling her anger. Her mother told her to take a hammer and nails, go out to the fence in the back yard, and hammer a nail into the wood every time she got mad. So the daughter did this each day. The first day she pounded a lot of nails.

Each day it became fewer and fewer nails as she learned to control her anger.

Soon the girl got to a point where she wasn't hammering any nails.

Her mother then told her to take a nail out for each day that she was able to hold her anger and constructively share her feelings.

Finally, all the nails were out of the fence. The girl had learned to control her anger. But the mother wasn't done. She took her daughter out to the slat fence. The mother complimented her daughter on learning to control her anger. She pointed to the remaining holes. The wooden fence will never be the same.

The wound is still there.

We live with the wounds that we cause, and we live with the harms caused by others. Both hurt. Into this milieu of damage, God offers healing:

Reverend Eugene Peterson's *The Message: The Bible in Contemporary Language* is a Bible translation, not of the original Hebrew and Greek words, but the meaning. Listen to *The Message*'s Hebrews 4:14-16:

> *Now that we know what we have — Jesus, this great high priest with ready access to God — let's not let it slip through our fingers. We don't have a priest who is out of touch with our reality. He's been through weakness and testing, experienced it all — all but the sin. So let's walk right up to him and get what he is so ready to give. Take the mercy, accept the help.*

I love this: *So let's walk right up to him and get what he is so ready to give. Take the mercy, accept the help.*

Do we have guilt and sin in our lives? Bring it to the throne. By Jesus' resurrection, we have forgiveness, mercy, and grace. In Jesus, we have a future without guilt.

Jesus' healing love is what makes this Good Friday. Originally "good" in this context meant holy. Holy Friday is Good Friday.

Today, we find in Jesus a new future with forgiveness and grace.

By Jesus' love, which he had even from the cross, we find a more powerful love than sin and death. Nothing is good about the crucifixion, but what is coming on Sunday will transform this evil event into good news for the entire world.

Jesus is good news for the world.

Jesus is healing all our wounds. Jesus is hope, peace, and new life for the entire world.

Amen.

Prayer:
Loving God, on this dark day, remind us of your presence. As we imagine Jesus' crucifixion, we are humbled. Be present, Lord. Nourish us with love. Feed us with hope. Strengthen us with peace. Infuse us with hope. Lord, on this Good Friday, we put our trust in you. In Jesus' name, we pray, Amen.

Easter
Acts 10:34-43

God Raised

> *Then Peter began to speak to them: "I truly understand that God shows no partiality, but in every nation anyone who fears him and does what is right is acceptable to him. You know the message he sent to the people of Israel, preaching peace by Jesus Christ — he is Lord of all. That message spread throughout Judea, beginning in Galilee after the baptism that John announced: how God anointed Jesus of Nazareth with the Holy Spirit and with power; how he went about doing good and healing all who were oppressed by the devil, for God was with him. We are witnesses to all that he did both in Judea and in Jerusalem. They put him to death by hanging him on a tree; but God raised him on the third day and allowed him to appear, not to all the people but to us who were chosen by God as witnesses, and who ate and drank with him after he rose from the dead. He commanded us to preach to the people and to testify that he is the one ordained by God as judge of the living and the dead. All the prophets testify about him that everyone who believes in him receives forgiveness of sins through his name."*

I had been waiting three years. I did not yet know about blockbuster movies, let alone sequels.

I was 11. I sat in the packed theater waiting through the two trailers before the screen showed the green "Feature Presentation" screen. Then everything went dark. And this was when the movie theater was *seriously* dark.

We waited.

John Williams' theme song for *Star Wars* began. Can you hear it?

It is early morning, and Mary, the mother of Jesus, and Mary Magdalene go to the tomb in the garden. They could not sleep much. They are *heart-shattered* with grief.

Just a week or so ago, they had no idea.

Jesus comes through Bethpage outside Jerusalem, where he climbs onto a young donkey for the ride into Jerusalem, the City of David. Jesus was welcomed — *welcomed* — into the city. Scores of Jews and some Gentiles coming out to put their cloaks and palm fronds down the road paving the way for Jesus their Christ, their Messiah, into the ancient holy city.

Here was Jesus entering Jerusalem. People cried out, *"hosanna."*

"Hosanna" means "Save."

Mary and Mary Magdalene are **broken,** remembering the people crying out for Jesus to save them. A week ago, the people celebrated Jesus as Messiah, the one they had been waiting for generations to arrive. They have been waiting for God to save them — just as their ancestors cried out for God to rescue them from slavery in Egypt — now they needed saving from the struggles of modern life.

Life can be challenging. People we love get sick. People struggle with love, with broken relationships, with random accidents that hurt and shatter. People have been wondering — "Where is God?" — amid this modern life we live.

Peter, in Acts 10, will preach Jesus to the world because he has had his eyes open. Peter sees. He sees Jesus at work in the world. Peter says:

> *Then Peter began to speak to them: "I truly understand that God shows no partiality, but in every nation, anyone who fears him and does what is right is acceptable to him. You know the message he sent to the people of Israel, preaching peace by Jesus Christ — he is Lord of all.*

Jesus is Lord of all. Who will have eyes to see? Who will listen and hear? Who will open their imagination?

Who will let the chills of a John William's score echo the heart-pounding feelings as we experience Easter as a visceral need for God?

We cry out for Jesus to save us.

Then one starry night in Bethlehem, Jesus came, born of a miracle in a small stable, for there was no room for them in the inn.

When Jesus is an adult, he will begin teaching, preaching, and healing throughout Judea and Galilee, even into Samaria. *Jesus went places, and Jesus changed lives.*

Jesus changed lives, and the word spread. People talked.

At the sheep's gate, Jesus asked the lame man, "Do you want to be made well?" Jesus took his hand, and he walked. (John 5:6-8)

Jesus felt his energy of love flow from him as the woman in twelve years of pain touched his cloak amid the crowd. He turned and conversed with her, which few would do as she was ritually unclean and unseen. Invisible. Jesus felt her presence. And the Holy Spirit healed her. Then Jesus forgave her sins. (Luke 8:43-48)

Jesus forgives our sins.

Joy has entered the world; laughter follows the changing of water into wine. (John 2:1-11) Jesus is fully on earth, calming the storms on the water and bringing joy and peace into people's lives. Jesus brings transformation to our lives.

Life gets better.

Then Jesus goes to Jerusalem, and the people cry out, "Hosanna, Save us!"

Mary, Jesus' mother, thought the people understood. Jesus was the Son of God, come to be with us — Emmanuel, God with us. Jesus is the Christ — the one who saves. Jesus' mother Mary thought the people understood!

Mary Magdalene, who had lived a life of violence and abuse, found hope for the future in Jesus. Jesus had cast seven demons from her life, and she followed him. (Luke 8:2) If the church fathers had been honest, she probably would have been included in the closest disciples. Instead, history conflates her with Mary, Lazarus and Martha's sister, who pours the perfume on Jesus' feet in John 12:1-8.

Mary Magdalene knew Jesus. Jesus saw her with love, without lust or judgment. He authentically saw her. And he loved who she was.

Jesus loved who Mary Magdalene could be.

Jesus' mother, Mary, thought people shouted "Hosanna" because they got it. Mary Magdalene was probably more realistic, but she still was hoping.

She hoped. This Sunday morning begins with everyone who knows Jesus, heart shattered.

Jesus loved people, even the Sanhedrin who conspired to have him executed. He loved Herod the Great, who wanted him dead. He loved the Roman governor Pilate, who found no crime but did not have the bravery to set Jesus free.

Jesus even loved Judas Iscariot, who he knew would betray him. Jesus sat at the table and shared the first communion with Judas. Did Jesus hope that Judas might let the communion change him? Did Jesus hope that Judas would let God save him?

Jesus prefers to keep loving Judas because Jesus always chooses to keep loving us no matter what we do, who we betray:

— who we gossip about, who we judge, how we hate,

— how we criticize, how we think we are better,

— how we divide the world between them and us.

God knows, Jesus knows, how the Holy Spirit wants to transform us so that we *finally see*. We finally see that there is no *us* or *them*.

Peter says (Acts 10:39-41):

> *We are witnesses to all that he did both in Judea and in Jerusalem. They put him to death by hanging him on a tree; but God raised him on the third day and allowed him to appear, not to all the people but to us who were chosen by God as witnesses, and who ate and drank with him after he rose from the dead.*

We are living in the dark tomb of fear, and God says, "No more!"

God rolled the stone away. *Hosanna*! The stone is rolled away so we can *be saved, transformed by love*. God lifts us with resurrection joy.

Mary and Mary Magdalene come to the tomb that first Easter morning and find the stone rolled away.

They see a gardener working nearby, and they ask him where Jesus' body has been taken. In Luke, they suddenly see an angel or two appear saying (Luke 24:5):

"Why do you look for the living among the dead? He is not here but has risen."

In the Gospel of John, chapter 20, Jesus' mother Mary, and Mary Magdalena, see the gardener but do not recognize Jesus, who says to them, "Family, why are you weeping? Whom are you looking for?"

Mary answers, and Jesus says, "Mary!" and she sees him.

When we sit waiting in the dark, waiting in the tomb, darkness becomes our eyes.

Then we must rely on our ears to listen.

To hear the good news of the gospel. Jesus dies on the cross, and God says, "No" to death and "Yes" to life.

God says we will have life and have it abundantly. When we think the darkness and evil are winning, we can turn to these resurrection stories and see that God is not finished yet.

God is not at all done with us, for there is life. Hosanna, Jesus has risen.

Jesus the Christ is risen and living. Friends, Jesus Christ, is risen today.

He is risen. He is risen indeed.

Amen.

Prayer:
Jesus Christ is risen today. Praise the Lord; the Lord's name be praised! Creator God, you have changed the world by love through the resurrection of Jesus Christ. We are thankful for Jesus in our lives. The Holy Spirit lifts us up, bringing peace to the world. Lord, we love and praise you in the name of the risen Christ — Jesus.

Easter Day
Colossians 3:1-4

Resurrection Power

> *So if you have been raised with Christ, seek the things that are above, where Christ is, seated at the right hand of God. Set your minds on things that are above, not on things that are on earth, for you have died, and your life is hidden with Christ in God. When Christ who is your life is revealed, then you also will be revealed with him in glory.*

Late Saturday, twenty-somethings are working out. I draw inspiration from them and kick discouragement to the curb.

Halfway through the workout, I sit at my least favorite machine: the leg press.

Getting into the machine always makes me feel like a goofy walrus.

Get into the machine. Adjust the seat. Legs up. Turn the lever to lock in my weight. I am feeling good to have moved into a new weight class. Let's do ten presses.

Press. No movement unless you count the muscle spasms in my back as absolutely nothing moves.

Sitting up, I see some joker has added a second lever to the bottom plate — 490 pounds.

Sometimes we do everything right, and nothing.

We press, we strain, nothing.

Does Easter have good news for us?

The disciples understand.

Brothers Peter and Andrew, James and John with Mother Mary, Mary, and Cleopas, and Philip, Judas Iscariot, and Judas Thaddeus called Jude. They have all been with Jesus for three years. They have come to believe Jesus as Messiah.

Then at the last meal they had with Jesus, Jesus told them that one at the table would betray him, without saying Judas' name. That night while praying, Jesus is arrested. Peter raises the dagger and cuts a man's ear off. Jesus heals it. (John 18:10)

Jesus heals someone who came to *arrest* him. Who does that? Who loves like that?

The disciples, the twelve, and the women and men who surround Jesus are weeping, mourning; some are heading back to the places from which they came because Jesus died on Friday.

Jesus died. What happened?

Then, in the gospel of John account, Mary Magdalene heads out early in the morning to the tomb where Jesus is buried. Maybe she goes to pray at the tomb.

And the stone is rolled away from the tomb.

The stone is rolled away for Mary Magdalene. *Not* for Jesus. Jesus did not need the stone to be moved. Mary Magdalene, who the gospels say met Jesus when he healed her of seven demons. That day, Jesus changed her life. And she followed him. That healing hinted at the resurrection power to come.

Resurrection power is now — Easter.

This power is beyond the earth's physics. Resurrection power has no limits, not even heavy stones sealing the tomb. Easter brings resurrection power, which is life over death itself. God says love will be the last word. Love is the first and last word and all the words in between.

John 1:14 says:

> *And the Word became flesh and lived among us, and we have seen his glory, the glory as of a father's only son, full of grace and truth.*

God raises Jesus Christ from death, energizing the resurrection power he had from the beginning, which he chose not to use so that as a human, Jesus could experience authentic human life. Jesus knows us, for he has lived the human life. God knows us.

Now, after three days with the dead, Jesus has broken the chains of death. Jesus is alive — full of resurrection power.

The Apostle Paul writing the letter to the Christian church in Colossae, says:

So, if you have been raised with Christ, seek the things that are above, where Christ is, seated at the right hand of God.

Seated at the right hand of God is power. Now that power is alive on earth this Easter morning. This resurrection power is here, active, and ready.

Our world needs this love-driven resurrection power.

For sometimes, life doesn't go right. The horror of Good Friday teaches us this. We remember such moments so that we can come on Easter morning to celebrate that love has the last word. Emmanuel, God with us.

Jesus is not dead. His resurrection power says he can pass solid doors. Jesus can come to wherever we are, wherever we need him. On the road to Emmaus, there Jesus was. Back at our fishing nets, there Jesus was. In the locked upper room, suddenly Jesus was there.

The massive stone was rolled away for Mary to see that Jesus' body was gone. Jesus was alive with resurrection power. Mary, Peter, and John could go inside, see the grave clothes, and believe with the stone rolled away.

Mary Magdalene believed. She was the first witness, the first preacher, telling Peter and John the tomb was empty. Peter and John ran to the open tomb while Mary stood outside weeping. "Why are you weeping?" the two angels asked. Mary answered:

they have taken away my lord, and I do not know where they have laid him. (John 20:13)

She told this to the angels, but in that holy moment, Jesus was suddenly here. Alive, fully human, fully God, physically present. And he said, "Why are you weeping?" (John 20:15)

And even Mary Magdalene didn't recognize him and went on about the body being missing. And then Jesus called her by name. "Mary!"

She (we) recognized him. Rabbouni, teacher!

Then the hugging. Like the return from the longest journey, the hug of great love. A hug that says you are amazing, I love you, I missed you, you are my family. We are family.

And what did Mary say next time she saw the disciples? "I have seen the Lord." (John 20:18)

I have seen the Lord.

This is the reality we live in on Easter morning. This is the reality; we live in an Easter world where Jesus is alive and active. With Jesus alive, we:

> *set our minds on things that are above, not on things that are on earth, for (we) have died, and (our) life is hidden with Christ in God.*

With resurrection power in our lives, the ministry we do reflects Jesus, not our own lives. Jesus Christ shines through us.

Yes, our lives do sometimes feel like the 490-pound leg press. We press, and nothing happens. Nothing happens without Jesus.

So press on with Jesus. Go with Jesus. Let the Lord Jesus lead us.

Jesus Christ is risen today!

Hallelujah, Amen.

Prayer:
Praise the Lord. The Lord's name be praised! Gracious and loving God, we celebrate the resurrection of our Lord Jesus Christ. Thank you for Jesus our Lord, our Savior, our resurrected king. Be with us this Easter day as we go forward as those prepared to live as your servants, loving the world in your name. We love and praise you, Jesus. Amen.

Easter 2
1 Peter 1:3-9

Evelyn Finds Hope

Blessed be the God and Father of our Lord Jesus Christ! By his great mercy he has given us a new birth into a living hope through the resurrection of Jesus Christ from the dead, and into an inheritance that is imperishable, undefiled, and unfading, kept in heaven for you, who are being protected by the power of God through faith for a salvation ready to be revealed in the last time. In this you rejoice, even if now for a little while you have had to suffer various trials, so that the genuineness of your faith — being more precious than gold that, though perishable, is tested by fire — may be found to result in praise and glory and honor when Jesus Christ is revealed. Although you have not seen him, you love him; and even though you do not see him now, you believe in him and rejoice with an indescribable and glorious joy, for you are receiving the outcome of your faith, the salvation of your souls.

One morning after worship, a mother wanted to share some news that was weighing her down.

Her twenty-something daughter Evelyn had been dating Andre. They had met in college in Toronto. It was a good relationship. Mom was so happy when Evelyn called to share the engagement news. She had been somewhat worried about them in that Andre didn't think the church was necessary. But that's normal for a lot of people, isn't it?

When Evelyn was visiting, Mom learned that Andre didn't want children. Evelyn explained that Andre's love of recycling and walking everywhere was part of his worries about the world. He didn't trust Ottawa and the Canadian government. He had many concerns about the world. Andre wasn't sure what kind of world would be around for any children they might have. Could they really bring children into a dying world?

Evelyn had asked mom what she thought of this. Mom said she threw up a quiet prayer for help before asking Evelyn what she thought. Did she see the world as dying as well? Did Evelyn want children?

Evelyn defended Andre's views, but then admitted she didn't hold them the same way. "But I'm a Christian, Mom. It's different for us."

It's different for us.

The Old Testament book of Joshua tells stories of the Israelites settling in the promised land. One of these stories is the story of the Battle of Jericho. (Joshua 6)

Jericho was hostile to the Israelites. The miraculous story of the Battle of Jericho involved God commanding the people of Israel to walk around the whole city every day. On the seventh day, they were to walk around the city seven times.

After the seven laps, they were to blow the horns, and the walls would fall.

How many Israelites believed this on the second, the third, and the fourth day walking around those walls? Was it hard to have faith when the townspeople of Jericho upon the walls rained down jeers and rotted fruit?

How much verbal abuse can you take and keep walking in faith? Did the number of Israelites walking decrease each day?

Did their leaders have doubts?

Andre had no faith in the future of the world. He had no faith in God, not believing in a living God. Evelyn said he thought there was a power for good at war with humanity's selfishness and narrow-mindedness. His few childhood experiences in hard wooden pews with loud preachers condemning him as a sinner who needed to come to Jesus did not convince him this Jesus was worth his trust.

When Evelyn and Andre visited Mom, he would sleep in as Evelyn and Mom went to church.

Andre had no faith; he had no hope.

Eight days after Easter Sunday, dare we say Andre is still living in the tomb? He is in complete denial that God has rolled the stone away. Andre puts on his Oakley® sunglasses at any hint of light cutting into the tomb of despair for the world.

When you don't believe in hope, you are not looking for it.

1 Peter 1 has good news, but it can be hard to hear as it is wrapped up in religious and church language. You almost need Google® translator to help understand what the missionary is saying to this Christian community. The Reverend Eugene Peterson brings clarity to 1 Peter 1:3-5 in *The Message:*

> *What a God we have! And how fortunate we are to have him, this Father of our Master Jesus! Because Jesus was raised from the dead, we've been given a brand-new life and have everything to live for, including a future in heaven — and the future starts now! God is keeping careful watch over us and the future. The day is coming when you'll have it all — life healed and whole.*

This is a great way to understand Easter, that Jesus' resurrection means:

> *we've been given a brand-new life and have everything to live for, including a future in heaven — and the future starts now!*

The good news is clear. 1 Peter encourages the church to know that God is with us, now and forever. God is here during any trials we face, so we are not alone in our suffering. God understands the hurt we feel.

God understands us. By the resurrection of Jesus, we can have life and have it abundantly both in the future, heaven but *also* right here on earth. We are *not* alone.

Jesus trusts our faithfulness. Our faithfulness isn't about getting it right all the time. Our failures, our sins and confessions of sins, our tripping on our own feet, our falling and getting back up, all of it will be rewarded. We can stumble in faith every day, none of this matters in the resurrection. It is our response to Jesus that matters. It is our "Yes, Lord, I'm listening" that opens us to the resurrection powers that Jesus offers to everyone.

Jesus' resurrection power is good news, for it can change the world. Jesus changes the world. He is transforming us from followers to disciples to servants of the world.

As forgiven people, we can live love and peace to the rest of the world — a world of Andres — who are still living in darkness. People who are stuck in the dark tomb. People who cannot see the light of the Lord amid their personal and societal worries.

Mom and Evelyn both understand what resurrection means. The world may not look like we want it to, but that isn't a call to give up. It is a call to arms. It is a call to push up our sleeves and get to work. God calls us through Jesus to be part of the restoration of our world. We are called to be part of the good work that God is doing.

The last straw for Andre and Evelyn was a mass shooting. This shooting struck home; it doesn't matter where it happened. They didn't know anyone involved, but it shook them.

Andre saw it as just more evidence that the world was on its last legs. He could not see any light, filled with hopelessness. The tomb was too dark.

Evelyn decided she needed a church and sought a Presbyterian Church of Canada congregation to be with on Sunday mornings. Andre took this as an insult to his beliefs. Evelyn didn't return to the church to spite Andre, she found a church because she needed the solace she found in the pews of that small congregation. She felt at home.

Later, she decided she wanted a life partner who knew hope too.

Andre and Evelyn amicably broke off their engagement. They still care for each other.

Evelyn knows what Easter means. She knows the world is not yet as it will be. Suffering continues. In her small church, she works to alleviate suffering by volunteering to do dishes with a group at the local monthly community meal and helping with the mid-high youth group. Evelyn remembers a lot of painful days from her own time in junior high.

Mom is thankful Evelyn is happy. She prays for Andre. Mom hopes he finds peace too.

Amen.

Prayer:
Dear Jesus, we are filled with the joy and glory of Easter. We know this world is not the way you wish it to be. Help us to work for our world's improvement. Help us value the creation, people at all economic levels, and people who believe differently from us. Gracious God give us more love for all the Andres of the world. Help us to listen to them and encourage them to see hope. You are a great God, and we trust in you, Amen.

Easter 3
1 Peter 1:17-23

The Alchemy Of Awkward

> *Since you call on a Father who judges each person's work impartially, live out your time as foreigners here in reverent fear. For you know that it was not with perishable things such as silver or gold that you were redeemed from the empty way of life handed down to you from your ancestors, but with the precious blood of Christ, a lamb without blemish or defect. He was chosen before the creation of the world, but was revealed in these last times for your sake. Through him you believe in God, who raised him from the dead and glorified him, and so your faith and hope are in God.*
>
> *Now that you have purified yourselves by obeying the truth so that you have sincere love for each other, love one another deeply, from the heart. For you have been born again, not of perishable seed, but of imperishable, through the living and enduring word of God. For, "All people are like grass, and all their glory is like the flowers of the field; the grass withers and the flowers fall, but the word of the Lord endures forever." And this is the word that was preached to you.*

Each time we have communion together, a strange ballet takes place.

Communion is about community. It is about a random group of people who have chosen to worship together, transformed from what we are — ordinary, sinful, confused — into God's people.

God's people. God is the creator of everything that was, is, and will be. We are God's people. This is not a minor miracle.

Communion is our transformation from who we are into the people we can become with God inside us. During communion, we *are* God's people.

Someone once said, "God loves us exactly the way we are, and God loves us too much to let us stay like this."[7]

All of this and more are happening when we are sharing communion.

As we pass the communion trays, an awkward transition is at play. We give the plate to our neighbor, and then as they hold it, we remove a piece of bread for ourselves. When the tray of little cups with wine or grape juice comes, again we pass it to our neighbor and, as they hold it, we take a cup for ourselves.

The theological intent of this awkward ballet is that no one is to serve themselves communion. It is always to be a communal act. People may find it easier to hold the plate in one hand and choose for themselves, but this meal isn't about what is easy.

Following Jesus is not easy. It isn't about being reasonable and finding the easy, wide-open road to walk. Faith is other people. Our church life is the practice of living God's way with these other people. Communion helps us learn these practices.

Something holy happens when you hold the plate of bread as I awkwardly remove a wafer for myself. Something sacred happens when I have the serving tray of cups, as you choose the perfect one for yourself.

Something holy happens in this awkward ballet of plate and cup.

One could say there is alchemy in the awkward.

Church life is filled with awkwardness. It is necessarily awkward for as Christians, we are living in a now and not yet kingdom. God is working to transform the world through us and the collective us — the church.

1 Peter 1 is a letter written to encourage the house churches in Asia Minor (modern Turkey) to be supported as they struggle with scorn and persecution. Our reading shows us that our faith isn't in gold or silver idols:

> *but with the precious blood of Christ, a lamb without blemish or defect. He was chosen before the creation of the world, but was revealed in these last times for your sake. Through*

---

7   Author unknown.

> *him you believe in God, who raised him from the dead and glorified him, and so your faith and hope are in God.*

Verse 21 is a powerful statement of hope. Jesus gives us faith to believe in the same God who raised Jesus from the dead and gave Jesus glory. In Jesus' glory, we find "our faith and hope in God."

During communion, we are transformed forward into the faithful people of God who can make a difference in the real world. 1 Peter is encouraging people not to live their best life locked behind doors in their house churches. The point is not to have a wonderful church life, but rather to learn how to be Christlike in church, then be like Jesus in the world.

The church is where we practice being like Jesus. We risk telling the whole truth. We learn to work with people who are socio-economically, politically, or theologically different from we are.

In the church, we have the auto mechanic sitting next to the software engineer, next to the stay-at-home dad, next to the person who will leave church with two bags of food from a shelf in the coatroom. And if this church is genuinely trying to be the kingdom of God, any of these people might be elders or deacons or Sunday school teachers or mission volunteers.

A church striving to truly reflect the kingdom of God has people of all walks of life in leadership and ministry.

Together we learn to respect and value each other. In communion, we live out this awkward alchemy as we practice serving each other.

Then the miracle comes. We forget the awkwardness as our neighbor says to us, "The Body of Christ, broken for you," and "The cup of salvation shed for you." Jesus Christ is alive in this awkward alchemy that transforms us into something new.

The alchemy of awkwardness is the transformation of regular people into the kingdom of God. We become the authentic Christian community.

Now the hard part comes. The Bible study ends. The community meals are complete. The finance meeting finishes. The worship service is over, the coffee pot is empty, and the cookie plate has crumbs.

Now we head to our cars. We walk home. We go out into the world to be Christians. We see if we can take the practices of faith we learn in the church and live authentic lives in the real world.

As we go, we remember the 1 Peter 1:24-25 blessing quoting Isaiah 40:8:

For, "All people are like grass, and all their glory is like the flowers of the field; the grass withers and the flowers fall, but the word of the Lord endures forever." And this is the word that was preached to you.

We may not get it right out in the world. But we will keep trying.

And whenever we gather for communion, we will practice the awkward alchemy of the bread and the cup. Once again, that unique alchemy of hope and love arrives. We are the kingdom of God.

We are the kingdom of God.

Amen.

Prayer:
The word of the Lord endures forever. Lord, we believe this. We put our trust in you. Be with us as we practice our faith in our churches and our homes. Give us strength to practice our faith in our workplace, our schools, and with our governments. Gracious Lord, be with us in all times and places. In Jesus' name, we pray, Amen.

Easter 4
1 Peter 2:19-25

Tennessee Red Mud

For it is a credit to you if, being aware of God, you endure pain while suffering unjustly. If you endure when you are beaten for doing wrong, what credit is that? But if you endure when you do right and suffer for it, you have God's approval. For to this you have been called, because Christ also suffered for you, leaving you an example, so that you should follow in his steps. "He committed no sin, and no deceit was found in his mouth." When he was abused, he did not return abuse; when he suffered, he did not threaten; but he entrusted himself to the one who judges justly. He himself bore our sins in his body on the cross, so that, free from sins, we might live for righteousness; by his wounds you have been healed. For you were going astray like sheep, but now you have returned to the shepherd and guardian of your souls.

Sometimes sitting up in the chancel during a worship service, I wonder about the stories of the people out in the seats.

We've sat in committee and board meetings. We've served side by side in youth ministry, on work projects, at vacation Bible school, and the annual all-day leaf rake to get the church grounds ready for winter. We have the chance to get to know each other.

One summer, a 180-member church spent every Tuesday and a few Saturdays working at Cass Community to clear a city block sized field of overgrowth and trash for a community green space. They cheerfully drove the ninety miles roundtrip to serve in Detroit. Those car rides and workdays were filled with conversations. We got to know each other well.

On one of those Saturdays, Sandra told me of her young adult children's difficulties with the church. They believe in God, love the people of their home church, but don't want to come on Sunday.

How much does it take to share these worries? We must be brave and willing to listen as people share their lives. They have stories of joy and heartbreak. We must listen.

At the end of a long international mission trip and after the last long talk with a hurting college leader, I stood on the path to my room and looked up at the night sky. I did some yoga breathing — some yoga praying. The stars were out. The ocean water twinkled with their light.

I prayed the Job prayers, "Why, God? Why?"

Sometimes all we can do is look at the stars and lay our burdens down at Jesus' feet.

Jesus understands. Jesus knows (1 Peter 2:23-24):

> *When (Jesus) was abused, he did not return abuse; when he suffered, he did not threaten; but he entrusted himself to the one who judges justly. He himself bore our sins in his body on the cross, so that, free from sins, we might live for righteousness; by his wounds you have been healed.*

Jesus, how did you do that? How did you find the love to "not return abuse" and "not threaten?" Sometimes I am so mad after hearing the stories of what evil people have done to people I know — to people sitting in these meetings, pews, homes.

Verse 25 convicts me in these times as I feel my anger lead me away from God's path:

> *For you were going astray like sheep, but now you have returned to the shepherd and guardian of your souls.*

I love this view of Jesus as the shepherd and guardian of our souls. When Christians care for other people, we may be risking a part of our soul to all the hurt and misery. We need Jesus to heal our souls from the anger that follows the painful stories.

At a Mids[8] youth conference down in Tennessee, I was wearing my brand new yellow conference t-shirt at Club Wreck — the afternoon game time.[9]

The relay involved fishing waders. One participant put on the waders, the team filled the waders with water, then the kid shuffled down to the other end where they climbed out of the waders, and another kid climbed in while other teammates tried to keep as much water as possible in the waders. Back the other way, repeat.

I was in the middle of the course, helping kids up when they fell.

I was focused on the team before me and never saw the kid from the next relay team who rammed into me from behind. I broke his fall as I face planted in the red Tennessee mud. He rolled off my back, found his feet, and kept going.

Mud from head to toe.

The red stain would not come out of that yellow conference t-shirt. It stayed in my drawer as I couldn't bear to throw it out.

How would our life be different if the sins in our lives were visible as stains on our clothes? What if our sins appeared on a flashing 4"x 4" screen on our left breast with a scrolling list of that year's sins? And the nasty stuff might be in bold print or with a prominent border of snakes?

What if we walked out with a digital version of Nathaniel Hawthorne's scarlet A from his 1850 novel *The Scarlet Letter*?

Would society be different?

I bet this would have a prominent effect on politics, teaching, and the church.

The church's nominating committee would have to refine its criteria for church leadership. Volatile people are out for children's ministry and deacon work. Liars are out for writing newsletters and teaching adult ed. Those of us clinging to anger over past failures and those of us who can't stop criticizing others will no longer be church ushers.

---

8   Mids or middle school ministry for 6th-8th graders
9   Yes, I did know better, but after two overnight fire alarms, my brain was not functioning at 6:30 am when my alarm started the day.

Now the church is empty.

An Instagram meme says, "The church is not full of hypocrites; there's room for one more."[10]

Months later, I pulled out the conference t-shirt to toss into my gym bag. I froze, holding the shirt up so I could see both sides.

The stain was gone. The shirt was yellow again.

The shirt was like new:

> (Jesus) bore our sins in his body on the cross, so that, free from sins, we might live for righteousness; by his wounds you have been healed.

In the Lord Jesus Christ, our sins are forgiven. We pray — confessing our sin, outing our lying, our hypocrisy, the hates we nurture, the anger that leads to hitting, the cheating. When we lay our sins down along with our burdens, Jesus is right here to receive them. Jesus forgives. Grace bathes us clean.

The church is full of sinners. It is full of forgiven sinners. Now we must go out and live such grace. We must live with love, joy, and peace in our hearts.

Our love should be visible when people see us. They should see our hope for the future.

They should be able to see that we care for them — right where they are. We care for the people we know, not so we can convince them to attend our brand of church, but because they are God's children.

Our focus should not be on their sin, for we are sinners too. Our focus needs to be like Jesus, who gathered a bunch of sinners — *People!* — around him and called them disciples. He gathered a bunch of sinners together and called them friends.

Jesus calls us too.

So come with your red-stained shirt, and meet Jesus.

Amen.

---

10 Author unknown.

Prayer:
Loving and forgiving God, thank you for your grace in our lives. We know that we are sinners in need of redemption. We know we don't follow you as we should. We don't love our neighbors, and sometimes we don't love ourselves. Forgive us. Redeem us, Savior. We love you, Amen.

**Easter 5
Mother's Day
1 Peter 2:2-10**

Bactine®

Like newborn infants, long for the pure, spiritual milk, so that by it you may grow into salvation — if indeed you have tasted that the Lord is good. Come to him, a living stone, though rejected by mortals yet chosen and precious in God's sight, and like living stones, let yourselves be built into a spiritual house, to be a holy priesthood, to offer spiritual sacrifices acceptable to God through Jesus Christ. For it stands in scripture: "See, I am laying in Zion a stone, a cornerstone chosen and precious; and whoever believes in him will not be put to shame." To you then who believe, he is precious, but for those who do not believe, "The stone that the builders rejected has become the very head of the corner," and "A stone that makes them stumble, and a rock that makes them fall."

Mother's Day, though not a Christian holiday, is significant. As Christians — as people of love — we want to say "thank you." More than this, we want to tell the people who raised us that we care for them.

It is about who raised us. Our moms may be our grandparents, a single father, an aunt and uncle, a single mother, or two parents together for many of us.

For some, Mother's Day is a joy with breakfast in bed or all the meals cooked by the family. It may be a fabulous brunch with a video chat with the extended family. Mother's Day might be a game of golf, a family hike, or a backyard picnic around the fire pit. Maybe your family piles in the car, traveling to your grandparents' house to celebrate generations of moms.

A Mother's Day centered on showing our care and thanksgiving is a good thing.

It can be a day we practice the love we experience in Christ Jesus. Jesus transforms us by his love:

> *Come to him, a living stone, though rejected by mortals yet chosen and precious in God's sight, and like living stones, let yourselves be built into a spiritual house, to be a holy priesthood, to offer spiritual sacrifices acceptable to God through Jesus Christ.*

Jesus can transform us into "spiritual houses" where we can live out love.

Mother's Day should be a glorious day of such love.

Sadly, for many, Mother's Day is painful. Some of us did not have healthy, nourishing relationships with our mothers. Others of us may be in pain as we actively grieve the recent death of our mother or of our child.[11]

Mother's Day can be just too painful.

As we've seen through our journey through 1 Peter, life can be tricky and painful. But 1 Peter is a letter of encouragement. God is with us when times are tough. By Jesus' death and resurrection, we know that nothing we face in our grief or difficult circumstances is something new to God. Jesus has faced it all.

Jesus understands our tears. 1 Peter 2:7 reminds us:

> *"The stone that the builders rejected has become the very head of the corner,"*

The religious leaders, with the crowds shouting "Barabbas," (Matthew 27:17) have rejected Jesus, but God through resurrection power has made Jesus the cornerstone of the future. Jesus is the cornerstone of the here — but not yet here — kingdom of God.

We are not alone. The resurrection power of Jesus can carry us through whatever circumstances we face. 1 Peter is full of encouragement for us to put our faith in Jesus. We are to trust that "by his wounds (we) have been healed." (1 Peter 2:24)

---

11 Active grief can take years, and three years is often considered average.

Growing up, my mom was the one I called when I got messed up. She would come with the green bottle that healed all my hurts.

When I think of the love I learned from my mother, I remember the smell of Bactine.

I was the kid constantly ramming about, climbing on stuff, and jumping off it. My mom was always reaching for the Bactine® — that 1970s magic spray that *stings*, cools, and heals.

With joy, I jumped off the dock and put my foot hard into the sandy bottom of Portage Lake, straight into a fishhook. We called over Mr. H, the nearest adult. He removed the hook with pliers as my mother hurried down from the cottage with the Bactine® in hand.

Out in the back, I climbed a tree, just to get a big sliver. Get the tweezers and pull — then Bactine®.

Bike riding down CK's driveway — flying down the steep hill, my front bike tire hit the sunken place below the street curb, giving me a 360-degree whirlwind tour of the driveway, sky and street. This one was a trip to urgent care in the old post office. Sometimes stitches are necessary. Mom used the stinging Bactine® each time she changed my bandage.

Yes, Mother's Day is a memory of Bactine® — memories of care, love, and kindness. Though I didn't understand it back then, these were some of my first experiences of Jesus Christ.

We all don't have a mom like mine, just as we don't have a mother like yours.

Sir Edwin Arnold wrote in his poem *Mothers*, "God can't always be everywhere, and so invented mothers."

1 Peter 2:6-7 reminds us that God intends to change the world through Jesus:

> *"See, I am laying in Zion a stone, a cornerstone chosen and precious; and whoever believes in him will not be put to shame." To you then who believe, he is precious…*

In last week's scripture lectionary reading, 1 Peter 2:25 reminds us:

For you were going astray like sheep, but now you have returned to the shepherd and guardian of your souls.

Jesus guides us back to God, who is the "guardian of (our) souls."

Jesus is the spiritual Bactine® that changes our lives. We can bring all of our hurts, worries, and emotional pain to Jesus to find healing. God intends healing for the distress and wounds that we face.

Such healing is possible on earth. Through Jesus in us, we believe God is moving the world to this deep healing — healing the wounds that separate us from one another. In Jesus, we experience the love that changes lives. It is a mother/father love that loves us through any hurt and separation we feel.

In Jesus is healing. In Jesus, Bactine® is no longer needed.

This healing is the big hug of someone who loves us with all their heart.

Praise the Lord. The Lord's name is praised. Amen.

Prayer:
Dear Jesus, we praise your name. We trust your resurrection power to lift us out of our troubles, reminding us that we are never alone. Thank you for all the people you have shared with us who love us unconditionally. We are so thankful for such love, Amen.

Easter 6
1 Peter 3:13-22

Baptized By Cool Water

Now who will harm you if you are eager to do what is good? But even if you do suffer for doing what is right, you are blessed. Do not fear what they fear, and do not be intimidated, but in your hearts sanctify Christ as Lord. Always be ready to make your defense to anyone who demands from you an accounting for the hope that is in you; yet do it with gentleness and reverence. Keep your conscience clear, so that, when you are maligned, those who abuse you for your good conduct in Christ may be put to shame.

For it is better to suffer for doing good, if suffering should be God's will, than to suffer for doing evil. For Christ also suffered for sins once for all, the righteous for the unrighteous, in order to bring you to God. He was put to death in the flesh, but made alive in the spirit, in which also he went and made a proclamation to the spirits in prison, who in former times did not obey, when God waited patiently in the days of Noah, during the building of the ark, in which a few, that is, eight persons, were saved through water. And baptism, which this prefigured, now saves you — not as a removal of dirt from the body, but as an appeal to God for a good conscience, through the resurrection of Jesus Christ, who has gone into heaven and is at the right hand of God, with angels, authorities, and powers made subject to him.

As the leader of my first international high school mission trip, I got to the airport before the 4 am check-in time for the 6 am flight. We were heading to Jamaica for work projects at the Caribbean Christian School for the Deaf (CCCD)'s Montego Bay campus.

I had never led an international mission trip, but I had led large summer camps and multiple youth trips to Tennessee under my belt. How different could it be?

On advice from the youth mission trip books, I had signed up for both the State Department's and CNN's email alerts about Jamaica.

Wow. Each week my email received reports of crime, storms, and poverty. Scary stuff!

One week, both warned us of thefts from tourist luggage in the Montego Bay airport. Jerry, the missionary to CCCD, confirmed this warning. He instructed us not to wear mission trip t-shirts through the airport and not even identify ourselves as such. Some of the previous youth groups wearing their team t-shirts had their luggage searched. Somebody had then stolen tools, supplies, and candy from the team's luggage.

Awesome.

We left Detroit in 65° June to land in hot Montego Bay. The air conditioners were out in the airport. The immigration line stretched forever; we inched along for over two hours. Live chickens squawked in cages.

The Welcome to Jamaica screens said the outdoor temperature was 96°. I tried not to think about the temperature in that long line.

As the trip leader, I put myself in cheerful, roll with it, church leader mode.

Sitting on the "I'm sure it's clean" floor in the custom's line, we played euchre. Euchre is a four-person card game played all over the Midwest in the long, dark winters.

Finally, my group, the last of our big group, cleared customs.

In the welcome area, my leaders and tired youth gathered around Jerry, who greeted me with a big smile holding up a torn notebook page on which he had written Pastor Monet. His smile was wide and as welcoming as his bright Hawaiian shirt. He was exuberant and not at all surprised at the late arrival.

Jerry would later explain that time was different in Jamaica. They had morning, afternoon, and night — that was enough, so enjoy the beauty of the people and the land.

Outside, the sun hit us. Jerry went to get the transportation which was quite a ways away. Just relax and enjoy being in Jamaica.

We waited with sweat dripping. We drank from our water bottles. Yum, warm.

Alice, a recent freshman on her first-ever mission trip, flopped onto a street bench. She screeched from the hot metal, jumped to the wooden end of the bench. She proclaimed in her best put-up-on-teenager voice, *"It's too hot, and I'm sick of it"*

Yes, we were in Jamaica — still at the airport — on the first day of a ten-day mission trip.

I tried to force myself to go over to her. And this is hard to admit, but I had nothing.

Have you been there? Have you been when you think you know what Jesus would do, but you just can't? You just can't. I had nothing to give: Alice wasn't wrong, it was hot. It had been a long day from the 4 am check-in to the flight change in Ft. Lauderdale, and the immigration waiting had dragged on forever. On top of all this, Montego Bay International Airport had been pure chaos everywhere. I was hot, tired, and feeling in over my head. As a Christian leader, I was praying, "Lord, help?" hoping to find the next gear of faithfulness.

Then, Molly, one of our rising seniors, headed over to Alice. Molly had been the exact age of Alice for the last international mission trip to the Yucatan. In the Yucatan, they slept in hammocks and washed from a five-gallon bucket for four nights during the workweek. Molly was an every-week teen at youth group. Surely, she would bring the encouragement.

Nope. Molly looked at her, and without compassion or even kindness, said, "If you think this is bad, you aren't going to like the workdays." Molly walked away.

Ouch.

The house churches in Asia Minor (modern Turkey) who suffer from persecution are at their wit's end. They need encouragement. The letters we know as 1 and 2 Peter are to be read during house church to bring a good word from the Christian missionaries. These people suffer from persecution for being Christian in a world that does not understand or respect Christians.

The people in these house churches are hot and thirsty. They are burning from the hard work of being loving in a hostile land, and they are thirsty for the cool water of the love of Jesus Christ.

They thirst for grace. They thirst for hope — for joy. They thirst to know that they are not alone.

1 Peter is a call to patience and perseverance. It is a reminder that in our baptism, we are changed. In Jesus, we are reborn by grace to love and tolerate those around us who do not know the good news of Jesus the Christ yet.

But these followers, these early Christians, are being persecuted. Possibly harassed, but it is still challenging to be a Christian. So each week, they gather in the house church to be encouraged and support each other.

Following Jesus was never promised to be easy. It was never going to be a walk in the park with smooth pavement, perfect shade trees, and a snow cone machine every 100 yards.

1 Peter 3:13 says:

Now who will harm you if you are eager to do what is good?

Listeners in the house church must have laughed at this. And possibly the reader of the letter is laughing right along with them. Maybe the Christian missionaries who have brought the letter to this house church are smiling as they present it.

Why are they laughing? This is funny stuff.

Now who will harm you if you are eager to do what is good?

Can you see that one great lady leaning into her husband, whispering in full snark, "Everyone!" Her husband shushes her. But a child hears and calls it out a bit louder. Soon the room erupts:

Who will harm us?

Everyone.

And just like that, the tension is broken.

Friends, we get it. Doing good isn't easy. Verse 14:

But even if you do suffer for doing what is right, you are blessed.

And the "you" here is plural. You, this church, will be blessed when you do what is right and good. Verses 18 and 21:

For Christ also suffered for sins once for all, the righteous for the unrighteous, in order to bring you to God

And baptism now saves you — not as removal of dirt from the body, but as an appeal to God for a good conscience, through the resurrection of Jesus Christ.

Baptism saves us.

Do we believe this? Baptism saves us.

The Lord Jesus Christ went to the cross loving his persecutors, even when we would have been reaching for our swords to fight the injustice. Instead, Jesus hangs on the cross and prays for those who persecute him. He prays for sinners like us. He prays, "Father forgive them for they don't know what they are doing." (Luke 33:34) Preach, Jesus, preach. We don't know what we are doing. But we know that Jesus loves us. And God so loved the world that He raised Jesus from the dead to break the power of sin and death in our lives.

Jesus' resurrection changes everything. Our baptism is the metaphoric/supernatural entrance into this rebirth of resurrection. In baptism, not only is the dirt washed away — everything that gets in the way of knowing and following Jesus has passed away. Jesus washes away all the bad in our lives while resurrection love splashes over us. We can love this world in all its messy harsh self.

We love the world because Jesus loves the world. We love the unlovable because Jesus loves them.

We arrived in Jamaica on a Saturday afternoon. The power would go out during worship. In the hills of Montego Bay, when the power goes out, the electric water pumps stop.

With all the work of getting the youth settled, meeting the beautiful people of the Caribbean Christian Center for the Deaf, learning to say my name in Jamaican sign language, I had chosen not to shower. Something to do before trying to sleep on a hot night. Bad decision.

No power meant no water and no shower.

I lay on my cot across from a recent college grad, one of our new leaders. It is hot. Our window has no screen, so the bugs have free access. We lay on top of our sheets covered in bug repellent goop. We try to sleep.

Monday morning, after a breakfast of Captain Crunch and fresh fruit, my team of seven young men and two amazing young women walked down the gravel drive to the bottom of the campus. Temperature is in the mid-90s at 8 am. We kept walking down to the bottom corner of the campus near the nine-foot walls.

Towering above us is a three-story classroom building. We've got one work team on top of it, building concrete block walls. Another group is in the cool shade at the lowest level, preparing to lay a new concrete floor over a mislaid base. Another mission team's work. Jerry said it was an adult team who didn't like the heat.

We had no shade or breeze in our corner of the campus.

We stood at the edge of a hole nine feet in diameter, six feet deep. We needed to dig it out to nine feet deep and nine feet in diameter — the new septic hole for the campus.

We did a short teaching time on the safe use of a pickax, always wearing safety goggles, and how to use a shovel effectively. Hot, half-asleep teenagers managed to find a way to roll their eyes.

We took an old wooden ladder and lowered it down. Jack and Rocko climbed down into the pit for the first shift. We pulled out the ladder, so they had some room.

"Hey, it's cooler down here," Rocko said. Then they started to dig.

The dirt went into a five-gallon bucket. A student would haul it up and pour it into a wheelbarrow. When the wheelbarrow was three-quarters full, a student would roll it up the hill to the team working on the new concrete floor who needed the fill dirt.

Every ten minutes, we swapped people in that hole. It got warmer. Gally and I climbed down the ladder when it was our turn. Everyone had lied — each rung down was another five degrees of hot. It was blistering in that sun-drenched hole.

Jack pulled the ladder out. Rocko suggested they all head to the beach now that they had me trapped in the hole. Everyone except Gally laughed, who looked at me silently, asking me to tell him that Rocko was kidding. I gave Gally the nod and smile. They were joking.

We put on safety goggles, took our pickaxes, and started alternate swings to break up that hard Jamaican dirt.

It was some of the most back-breaking work I have done in over 35 mission trips since. It was also some of the worst heat of my life.

When Gally was cooked, he quietly asked me if we could stop. I waved to Jack to send the ladder down, saying we were done. Gally crawled up the ladder. I followed, collapsing in the grass. Jack and Rocko descended for their next time.

Every so often, someone would take our water bottles over to the faucet outside the dorms. They would refill the bottles with fresh spring water. When they returned, they would hand me my bottle, and I would open the top and take a long swallow of cool holy water.

That cool water was resurrection itself.

Why do we follow Jesus when it gets hard? Why follow Jesus when it would be easier to just not?

We follow God for that cool water of Jesus. The cool, life-giving water baptizes us.

Amen.

Prayer:
Dear Lord, thank you. Thank you for the small acts of kindness that make life better. We thank you for the people who changed our diapers, the ones who woke up in the middle of the night to feed us or sit with us when we were ill. We thank you for people who say "hello" each day when we arrive. We thank you for people who write notes and mail them, as well as those who, out of the blue, text us with a "thinking of you" meme. Dear Lord, thank you for the little joys of fresh spring water. Thank you for Jesus, Amen.

Ascension of the Lord
Ephesians 1:15-23

Christ's Body On Earth

I have heard of your faith in the Lord Jesus and your love toward all the saints, and for this reason I do not cease to give thanks for you as I remember you in my prayers. I pray that the God of our Lord Jesus Christ, the Father of glory, may give you a spirit of wisdom and revelation as you come to know him, so that, with the eyes of your heart enlightened, you may know what is the hope to which he has called you, what are the riches of his glorious inheritance among the saints, and what is the immeasurable greatness of his power for us who believe, according to the working of his great power.

God put this power to work in Christ when he raised him from the dead and seated him at his right hand in the heavenly places, far above all rule and authority and power and dominion, and above every name that is named, not only in this age but also in the age to come. And he has put all things under his feet and has made him the head over all things for the church, which is his body, the fullness of him who fills all in all.

What a beautiful way to begin a letter to the Christian churches in the Greek city of Ephesus: *I have heard of your faith in the Lord Jesus and your love toward all the saints....*

Isn't this beautiful?

You are a devoted congregation. People have shared with the disciples how faithful you are. People have been talking about how the Christians in Ephesus maintain the Christian faith amid so much decadence in Ephesus, the occult capital.[12]

The Ephesian Christians stand firm to the difficulties of following Jesus in a community that does not value their faith or

12 See description of Ephesus in Lent 4 — "Shine Bright."

even their God. Scholars have theorized that the Ephesians community would have been critical of the Christian and the Jewish communities for their rejection of their neighbors' plethora of gods. It is customary to worship a god for the crops, another for fertility, and the third god for health. The belief that there is only one God was new to them and strange.

Meanwhile, for the Christian house churches, the people learn who God is through the letters they are receiving from the missionaries. Theology is changing in real-time for the church. The churches might have had access to the gospel of Mark, but Matthew, Luke, and John's gospels may not yet have been written.[13] Scholars date the book of Ephesians to somewhere between 80 and 90 AD.

These Christians in their house churches had to focus on the essentials — faith, hope, baptism, communion, confession/forgiveness — all through the life, ministry, death, and resurrection of the Lord Jesus Christ. Ephesians 1:17 is encouragement for the community:

> *I pray that the God of our Lord Jesus Christ, the Father of glory, may give you a spirit of wisdom and revelation as you come to know him, so that, with the eyes of your heart enlightened, you may know what is the hope to which he has called you...*

This is a powerful prayer for the Christian community. It is a prayer that "God... the Father of glory" will send "wisdom" and "revelation."

Biblical wisdom, as described in the Old Testament, is an astuteness for making good life decisions. This wisdom connects with Torah — the Law — which brings intelligence and knowledge from God.

Revelation is similarly understood to come from God. Revelation is a supernatural opening of the curtain to see the world from God's point of view. The word comes from the root of uncovering.

---

13 Scholarly debate of the dating of the books of the Bible is constant. The key is that the Ephesian churches had firsthand accounts of the events of Jesus life and the missionary work of the disciples.

The author of the letter to the Ephesians is powerfully praying that these house churches will experience God's wisdom and revelation so that they can see the best way to be as people and churches in their communities.

This wisdom and revelation come through faith in Jesus Christ "when he raised him from the dead and seated him at his right hand in the heavenly places…" (Ephesians 1:20)

See how this proclamation goes straight from death to seated at God's right hand? The writer skips all the resurrected appearances to intensify the theological assertion that Jesus went from dead to resurrected to sitting at the right hand of God.

It is vital for the Ephesians' churches that Jesus is seated in power.

All the churches of Asia Minor, Egypt, and everywhere in the Roman empire should not be looking for a physical Jesus. Jesus has ascended to heaven. God has raised Jesus not only from the dead but up to the heavenly realm.

Jesus is indeed King of kings now.

Acts 1:7-11 tells of Jesus ascension to the throne:

> *(Jesus) replied, "It is not for you to know the times or periods that the Father has set by his own authority. But you will receive power when the Holy Spirit has come upon you; and you will be my witnesses in Jerusalem, in all Judea and Samaria, and to the ends of the earth."*
>
> *When he had said this, as they were watching, he was lifted up, and a cloud took him out of their sight. While he was going and they were gazing up toward heaven, suddenly two men in white robes stood by them. They said, "Men of Galilee, why do you stand looking up toward heaven? This Jesus, who has been taken up from you into heaven, will come in the same way as you saw him go into heaven."*

The Ephesian churches may not have had the written Acts account, but they certainly had oral tellings of Jesus' ascension.

A part of these ascension stories would be Jesus promise of the Holy Spirit:

But you will receive power when the Holy Spirit has come upon you; and you will be my witnesses in Jerusalem, in all Judea and Samaria, and to the ends of the earth."

Along with the ascension stories, they have the Pentecost stories (Acts 2) of the miracle of the Holy Spirit arriving as tongues of fire into the center of Jerusalem.

Jesus up in the heavenly realm and the Holy Spirit here on earth are meant to strengthen our faith. They are a reminder that Jesus' resurrection power is active and robust. Jesus is:

far above all rule and authority and power and dominion, and above every name that is named, not only in this age but also in the age to come. And he has put all things under his feet and has made him the head over all things for the church, which is his body, the fullness of him who fills all in all.

The Ephesians churches are part of Christ's body on earth.

Our churches today are part of Christ's body on earth.

The "fullness of him" is an interesting phrase that one might translate as the "completeness of him."

Could this phrase mean that as we grow spiritually and our churches grow with new believers, Jesus becomes complete? This isn't to say that Jesus is incomplete in a lessened form. Rather, it is like our Thanksgiving table is better when family, friends, and neighbors sit together. The table is so full because we went out and invited everyone to come to be together.

Jesus is complete when our churches have opened doors and a truly authentic community for everyone.

Who do we invite? Everyone. Who is welcome? Everyone. Even...? Yes, they are part of everyone.

The Ephesians' churches should keep sharing the good news of Jesus Christ with the people of their community. They should do so with love.

We should keep sharing the good news of Jesus Christ with the people of our community. We should do so with love.

Praise the Lord. God's name be praised.

Prayer:

We worship you, Lord Jesus. We adore you, Loving Spirit. We honor you, creator God. Walk with us here on earth. Bring the resurrection power of Jesus here to live in our lives through love, peace, and joy. We trust in you with our whole lives, Amen.

Seventh Sunday of Easter
1 Peter 4:12-16, 5:6-11

Lava Faith

> *Beloved, do not be surprised at the fiery ordeal that is taking place among you to test you, as though something strange were happening to you. But rejoice insofar as you are sharing Christ's sufferings, so that you may also be glad and shout for joy when his glory is revealed. If you are reviled for the name of Christ, you are blessed, because the spirit of glory, which is the Spirit of God, is resting on you. But let none of you suffer as a murderer, a thief, a criminal, or even as a mischief-maker. Yet if any of you suffers as a Christian, do not consider it a disgrace, but glorify God because you bear this name.*
>
> *Humble yourselves therefore under the mighty hand of God, so that he may exalt you in due time. Cast all your anxiety on him, because he cares for you. Discipline yourselves, keep alert. Like a roaring lion, your adversary the devil prowls around, looking for someone to devour. Resist him, steadfast in your faith, for you know that your brothers and sisters in all the world are undergoing the same kinds of suffering. And after you have suffered for a little while, the God of all grace, who has called you to his eternal glory in Christ, will himself restore, support, strengthen, and establish you. To him be the power forever and ever. Amen.*

During my sophomore year at Hope College, I lived with seven guys who were graduating that May. I knew a couple of the guys already and got to meet so many new people. Our house was in a central location on campus, so people stopped by often.

Most were cool people — most.

One stands out even now. Every time this guy came to our house, he introduced himself again as if we had not met. Every time he shared that he was pre-med.

Ooh.

Right before their graduation, he came bursting through our front door in a lather, bursting with righteous indignation.

His father did not understand him. His father did not *get him*. His well-meaning but clueless father had given him a convertible for graduation, and — hold on — it was blue!

Blue, can you believe it? Everyone knows red is better.

I wish I could tell you that he was kidding. He was not. He was furious that his dad had been so unthinking.

My parents had gone through a messy divorce the year before; communication with my dad was spotty at best. As I listened to this guy go on and on, my blood boiled. I bit my tongue, stood up, and bolted from the house. I did not stop to breathe until I was blocks away, passing a Christian Reformed Church.

Standing outside that church, I gasped a prayer to God.

Have you prayed in gasps? It is prayer without words as your broken heart — your angry heart — spews emotions toward the *one who loves*. Sometimes words are involved. Some may be blue or even four-letter. The book of Jeremiah, chapter 20, tells us that when the prophet Jeremiah was beaten and locked in the stocks upon his release, he prayed a poem of pain in which he cursed his birth.

Yes, Jeremiah knew about gasping prayers. In Jeremiah 38, men lower Jeremiah by rope into a cistern (Jeremiah 38:6):

> *Now there was no water in the cistern, but only mud, and Jeremiah sank in the mud.*

Jeremiah probably gasped out his prayer while sitting in the hot, stinky well, down in the mud, thirsty with no accessible water to drink. Following God was not easy.

Yes, Jeremiah knew gasping prayers.

I bet some of you do too.

> *Beloved, do not be surprised at the fiery ordeal that is taking place among you to test you, as though something strange were happening to you.*

1 Peter may be a sermon in chapters 1-3, but then chapters 4 and 5 are full of encouragement to have patience, to persevere, and let the struggle strengthen our faith.

I love the visual language used throughout 1 Peter 4 and 5.

"Fiery ordeal" is not to be taken literally, but always remember that the worst feeling to people living in a desert is thirst. The fiery ordeal, or as it is in the Old Testament and quoted in the gospels, the lake of fire, is the worst thing you can have for desert people. First, you are hot and thirsty. Second, everything gets worse, and now you are not just typically hot and thirsty, but experiencing unending thirst as if you are sailing on a lake of fire.

Sailing a lake of fire is a fiery ordeal that, visually and symbolically, gets at the heart of what it is like to be separated from the love and communion of our Holy God — being alone. Suffering.

The house churches where Christians meet for worship are where the people gather to support each other. Together they can get through anything. They can persevere together:

> (D)o not be surprised at the fiery ordeal that is taking place among you to test you, as though something strange were happening to you. But rejoice insofar as you are sharing Christ's sufferings, so that you may also be glad and shout for joy when his glory is revealed.

Friends, this test isn't from God. Suffering isn't a test from God.

Much suffering comes from things we do to hurt ourselves and the ones we love. We work too many hours, missing out on home life. We use sarcasm without a thought about how it makes people feel. We lie to avoid uncomfortable conversations, even as though lies damage our relationships.

Sometimes our suffering comes from the vagaries and accidents that just happen. A car runs the stop sign while we are biking in the intersection. We hit the diving board during a flip. The sewer water floods the basement, destroying heirlooms and baby photos. The doctor wants to discuss the colonoscopy results.

Last, and often worst, is the suffering from people who choose hate and sin, inflicting hurt on us. Some people derail our lives with their evil actions.

People suffer.

God does not want us to face misery alone. 1 Peter 4:16:

Yet if any of you suffers as a Christian, do not consider it a disgrace, but glorify God because you bear this name.

The "you" in all this is plural. We suffer together. We are the house church. We gather to be together, worship almighty God, and experience God's healing. Jesus restores us. Now we can show love amid the suffering. We can reflect Jesus to the world. 1 Peter 5:7, 10-11:

Cast all your anxiety on him, because he cares for you.
And after you have suffered for a little while, the God of all grace, who has called you to his eternal glory in Christ, will himself restore, support, strengthen, and establish you. To him be the power forever and ever, Amen.

I love this blessing in verse 11: *To him be the power forever and ever, Amen.*

Harper's Bible Dictionary defines "amen" as "certainty, truthfulness or faithfulness."[14] Amen means "let it be so" or "it is so." 1 Peter 5:11 is an incredible blessing as it proclaims that Jesus Christ is worthy of all *power forever and ever, Amen, AND let it be so.*

God knows we suffer sometimes. God listens with compassion and love when we gasp out our prayer from that pain of fiery pain deep in our hearts. God knows. We *are* not alone.

Each week when we gather in the church: be it in an Ephesian house church, a small rural congregation, a 1980s-megachurch, a magnificent gothic cathedral, or, as 2020-2021 taught us to be together online in the digital spaces — in any of these,

---

14 The Society of Biblical Literature, ed. Paul J. Achtemeier, Harper's Bible Dictionary (New York: Harper & Row Publishers, Inc., 1985), 26.

we assemble to be the church. We build community. In our faith community, we gather not to be alone.

Together we build a lava faith.

One of my favorite games as a kid was playing the floor is lava. My mom did not approve.

For lava, we would see if we could circle our family room without touching the floor, or lava. Pillows became rocks to jump over to escape the lava floor. Chairs were mountains to climb. This game was so much fun with my older brother and a few friends.

Sometimes I would try to play lava alone, but it was boring alone. Friends made lava better.

I can't make it! Take my hand. I'll pull you over.

Grab my hand. I've got you.

We are not alone. To Jesus, be the power forever and ever. Amen. Let it be so.

Prayer:
God of the desert and the fiery places, meet us wherever we are. God of the lake and the lava, pour for us the cool, spring water that heals us. We trust in Jesus Christ, the living water. We know that by the Holy Spirit we are never alone. Bring your sustaining love to our lives so that we might go forth boldly to love this world in your name, Amen.

CPSIA information can be obtained
at www.ICGtesting.com
Printed in the USA
BVHW040225060223
657960BV00005B/93